The Beginner's Guide to the Prophetic

The ABC's of Personal Prophecy

Matthew Robert Payne

Copyright © Matthew Robert Payne 2016 All rights reserved.

No part of this publication may be reproduced, stored in a retrieval system or transmitted in any way by any means, electronic, mechanical, photocopy, recording or otherwise without the prior permission of the author except as provided by USA copyright law.

All scriptures are taken from the New King James Version unless otherwise noted.

Scripture taken from the New King James Version®. Copyright © 1982 by Thomas Nelson. Used by permission. All rights reserved.

Holy Bible, New Living Translation, copyright © 1996, 2004, 2015 by Tyndale House Foundation. Used by permission of Tyndale House Publishers Inc., Carol Stream, Illinois 60188. All rights reserved.

King James Version (KJV). Public Domain.

You can contact Matthew Robert Payne at survivors.sanctuary@gmail.com

To support my ministry or request a personal prophecy, see my website at http://personal-prophecy-today.com

You can find my published books on my Amazon author page here:

http://tinyurl.com/jq3h893

Editor: Lisa Thompson — For your editing needs, contact Lisa at www.writebylisa.com or at writebylisa@gmail.com.

The opinions expressed by the author are not necessarily those of Revival Waves of Glory Books & Publishing.

Revival Waves of Glory Books & Publishing
PO Box 596
Litchfield, IL 62056
United States of America
www.revivalwavesofgloryministries.com

Revival Waves of Glory Books & Publishing is committed to excellence in the publishing industry.

Published in the United States of America

Paperback: 978-1-365-75997-0

Table of Contents

Dedication 4

Acknowledgements 5

Foreword 8

Introduction 11

Chapter 1 Personal Prophecy - What Is It? 13

Chapter 2 Being Prophetic - What Is That? 23

Chapter 3 What Is a Prophetic Person, and What Is a Prophet? 37

Chapter 4 What Are Some Keys to a Prophet's Life? 49

Chapter 5 How Do I Know if I Am Called to Be a Prophet? 62

Chapter 6 How Is Personal Prophecy Useful? 73

Chapter 7 Nine Purposes of Personal Prophecy 81

Chapter 8 Eight More Purposes of Personal Prophecy 96

Chapter 9 Nine Benefits of Personal Prophecy 106

Chapter 10 Being the Light of the World 128

Closing Thoughts 142

Author Bio 143

I Would Love to Hear from You 144

How to Sponsor a Book Project 145

Other Books by Matthew Robert Payne 146

Dedication

To my best friend in the world, one who is closer than a brother, Jesus Christ.

Acknowledgements

June Payne

I want to thank my mother for listening to me as I talked about writing this book with her out loud. Putting a book together takes a lot of patience. My mother was my sounding board through the whole process.

The Workers at Fiverr

I want to thank the typist who faithfully and efficiently typed out all of the videos that comprised this book. She did a wonderful job, and I could not have done this book without her.

I want to thank the graphic artist at Fiverr who designed my book cover. I have worked with him on seven covers now, and he always does a great job. I am so pleased that my book writing ministry can give work to others.

Liz Philpott

I want to thank Liz for a generous donation that made it possible for me to hire a very good editor for this project.

Bill Vincent of Revival Waves of Glory Books and Publishing

I want to thank Bill for preparing and publishing this book, the eighth one that we have worked on together. Bill works tirelessly to do his very best for authors who want to self-publish. Bill is more than a publisher; he is a successful apostle who has stewarded three revivals. By using his services to publish your book, you are really supporting the work of the Lord.

The Readers

I want to thank the readers who motivated me to write this book, which is to educate them and not to make money. I made an effort to really explain my heart in regards to the prophetic and tried to make it easy for a beginner to understand. Even so, this book takes you into solid food beyond just milk. I am very happy with how it has turned out, and I pray that you will learn from it.

Jesus Christ

Jesus, I want to thank you for being my friend. You have been with me through all my life, my years of sinful behavior and through all my growth. You have been so good to me. It is with your permission and love for me that I have been blessed to produce this book to equip people.

Holy Spirit

Thank you for leading me and being such an active part of my life and directing me each day. Thank you for leading me to the right books to read, for teaching me and for giving me my anointing and gifts. You are my champion. Thank you.

Father

I am just now beginning to get to know you in a deeper way. Thank you for giving me your son for all these years of my life. Thank you for being so patient with me, waiting for me to come to you and to get to know you. I pray that this book will bless thousands of people.

Foreword

I have known Matthew Robert Payne for some years and consider him a friend. I was so honored when he asked me to write the foreword for this informative endeavor into the realm of the prophetic. He has written some fabulous books regarding prophetic ministry.

As I read through this particular book, I was impressed with the regard that he gives to the instruction of emerging prophets and prophetic people. He does so in a way that makes it easy for those entering into this particular realm to comprehend. His clear-cut writing style and reader-friendly structure makes "A Beginner's Guide to the Prophetic" a must read for anyone interested in the subject. People who know me know that prophetic ministry is my passion. Matthew is the same way. He is fervent about its expansion and its impact upon the next generation.

This book will take you on a journey through authentic, God-ordained issues that many face in order to transition into becoming prophetic people. Matthew gives an illuminating perspective to an often maligned and misunderstood gift that is readily available to any Holy Ghost filled believer. In Numbers 11, Moses stated that, "Enviest thou for my sake? Would God that all the Lord's people were prophets and that the Lord would put His Spirit upon them!" God's desire is that we are all prophetic! This gift is not just for the prophet, but for you as well. This labor of love by Matthew Robert Payne will speak to a new generation of seers. It will help them identify their gift, use it and impart it to others.

Each component of this journey has a significant part. Significance is defined as the meaning to be found in words or events. This writing is significant! Throughout this manuscript, each chapter represents an important part of the whole. The chapters build upon each other, like the bricks of a house, to structure an exact design that is found within the words of the writer. Like laying a foundation, you will begin on the ground floor of transition into the prophetic, establishing an edifice. The book provides depth built upon the foundation of the author's own personal journey, which may very well resonate with your own. It will equip you with an understanding of how to deal with your own proverbial bumps in the road within the realm of the prophetic.

Matthew shares his journey with courageous authenticity, and you can likely relate to the instruction that he shares, birthed in the wilderness of isolation. Isaiah 10:27 tells us that the anointing removes burdens and destroys yokes. Oil represents the anointing. The oil on this book comes from God and rests on the author. The anointing costs each of us something dear, and Matthew has paid a tremendous price for the wisdom that rests within the pages of this book. As his friend, I personally know of some of the obstacles he has faced in his life. I am aware of the hard path of his journey and how God has truly brought Matthew to the place in the spirit where he is now. As you read this book, you will experience the agape that he has for God's people, especially his emerging prophets.

Dr. John Veal
Senior Pastor of Enduring Faith Christian Center
CEO of John Veal Ministries

Introduction

To be called as a prophet is a tall order. While many people may see it as a privileged and glamorous lifestyle, being a prophet means hard work and will take an emotional and spiritual toll on your life.

This book will suit you if you think that you are called to be a prophet. You may have just thought about it, or you may have had a few people prophesy your destiny over your life. I don't imagine this will be the last book that you will ever read on the prophetic, but if it is the first one, it is a good, basic primer for you.

One of the major things that you will be doing as a prophet is to deliver personal prophecies to people. This book takes a good look at personal prophecy and how it can be valuable and beneficial to people.

It is my prayer that you will not run from your calling like Jonah and that you will stay the course over the next 10 to 25 years that it will take for you to mature into the office of prophet. This is not a textbook, and it is not full of scriptures, but it is a simple guide for you to get a feel about the ministry office to which you will belong.

If you are just prophetic and do not have a calling to be a prophet, the chapters on prophecy will be useful to you.

Some books are long on factual information and short on personal testimony. I hope that you find this book both factual and filled with enough testimony so that you have a good idea of what sort of prophet I am.

Enjoy!

>Matthew Robert Payne
>March 2016

Chapter 1
Personal Prophecy - What Is It?

To start, let me say that the world has become accustomed to the supernatural. People who aren't Christians understand that if they want to know their life's purpose, if they want to know about love, if they want to know about jobs or if they want to know about their future, they can quite happily ring a psychic line or visit a clairvoyant for a tarot card reading. They know that they can have their palms read for information about their life, their challenges, the things they want and their future.

The world is open to the supernatural and fascinated with life as people want to know their purpose and their future. People of the world, no matter how average, want to find information on things that are important to them like love, relationships, money, jobs, career, their future, their purpose and their destiny. The adventurous and curious will seek answers in the occult, but little does the world know that prophetic people can supply these same answers for them.

We live in a world of mystery; we're given this life, and we all arrive without any knowledge of what it is supposed to look like. Both non-believers and Christians want to know about their life, their future and purpose for living.

Andrew Wommack is a popular Christian teacher on Christian television who has written dozens of books. He conducts seminars in cities around the U.S. and teaches on life's purpose and destiny. When he teaches, he asks people to come forward if they don't know what their life's purpose is. He reports that about 80 percent of the Christians present come forward. It's very sad if you are a Christian living on earth who does not yet know why you're here.

When we are born as babies, we don't know anything. We grow up, get saved and become a Christian, but we still don't know who we are meant to be. We can pursue things that we seem to like. We can decide when we're young that we want to be an accountant or a builder or a lawyer. We can study further, take technical courses and attend college to equip ourselves for what we think we're meant to be doing, but so many people are still living in this world without answers. Most are just facing each day as it comes, putting one foot in front of another in a purposeless, directionless existence.

An effective prophetic person can solve this problem for people.

1 Corinthians 12 mentions the nine gifts of the Holy Spirit. Many gifts can be utilized with prophecy, but the three main gifts that relate to prophecy in this chapter are prophecy itself, the word of knowledge and the word of wisdom. These three prophetic gifts work together to form what we know as a personal prophecy. Someone who gives a personal prophecy

is giving information to a person about their past, present and future life.

Through prophecy, God supernaturally reveals information for a person to understand:

- God's love for them
- Their direction in life
- Their purpose in life
- The ways that God really views them and
- What God really thinks of them.

A prophecy is given to encourage, edify and exhort people. We're meant to be built up with personal prophecy. A person should be able to get a handle on what they are meant to do with their life through prophetic ministry.

Prophecy is never meant to be judgmental or discouraging to a person. You should never come away from a personal prophecy feeling down, sad, depressed, condemned or guilty. Anyone who delivers a personal prophecy that brings shame, condemnation or guilt to a person hasn't acted according to the Spirit of God and hasn't delivered a prophecy correctly.

Let's talk about the basics of personal prophecy. For example, here are a few things personal prophecy might say, including things that God likes about me:

- He sees me as very humble.
- I have a teachable spirit.
- I have a childlike faith.
- I'm a person of resilience.
- I'm a person with perseverance and
- I'm very patient.

God has spoken about all of these qualities to me on multiple occasions in the past. I know that this is how God sees me. God sees who you are and communicates it through the mouth of a prophetic person. Over time, with more and more prophecies that you receive from a prophetic person or a prophet, you build a portfolio of what God thinks of you, the character traits that he likes about you and who you really are.

We live in a carnal world where people measure success according to money and to personal happiness. People gauge your worth according to your biological family, the clothes that you wear, the cars that you drive and the house that you own. We should not measure people's success by their possessions. Nor should we do it through their level of understanding of the Bible.

Some people feel ashamed if they come from a position of financial struggles. They may have come from a church that didn't teach much of the Bible. These people from poor families who don't have a full understanding of the Christian faith and who don't understand who God is can feel left out. They can suffer and not prosper in life as all these things weigh against them, and they can feel unwanted. They can feel rejected and humiliated in front of other people.

These people need to be told that they're special and that they were selected and chosen by God. They need to be told that they have a life purpose and that even the worst things that have happened to them can be overcome through the grace of God. Prophecy is simply a vehicle that can demonstrate and tell a person who they are to God, not based on man's assumptions or opinions that we get from living in this carnal world.

Through prophetic ministry, these poor people can get a picture of God's true perspective of who they are. Prophecy can encourage a person and give direction. It can act a little like an investigative journalist who zeroes in to find the trouble and trauma that happened to the person. God can reveal a trauma or a bad experience through a word of knowledge, which is supernatural information.

God can reveal a hidden distress in a prophecy, and the person can realize that God understands their pain and suffering. They can be given a prophetic promise that God is going to restore and heal them. They can be told that God is going to put their feet on solid ground and use their testimony to lead others into success and prosperity.

If you don't believe that is possible, then my life and story stands out as an example of how it can happen.

Prophecy is amazing, and Christians are not the only ones who can prophesy. Everyone is born with gifts, natural talents and supernatural abilities. People with these gifts and abilities who aren't Christians become psychics and clairvoyants. They can receive supernatural information about a person's past and trauma, destiny, future and their purpose; what they love; and what they're destined to do. These people can be alarmingly accurate.

They believe that the source of their prophecies is an ascended master or a spirit guide, generally someone who achieved a certain spiritual progress on earth. Now, they believe that when these spirit guides crossed over to what they call the "other side," they're communicating and counseling people who are still living and giving them directions and spiritual insight. Clairvoyants or mediums who get information from a spirit guide do not believe that they're doing anything evil.

They believe that someone spiritual on the other side of life is giving those insights and counsel for people's lives. This is not true. The average clairvoyant wouldn't see themselves as a satan worshiper or as evil but is a beautiful person who is gifted, knows it and simply wants to help people through their gift.

Some of them may charge for services, but many clairvoyants and psychics just love their gift and will minister freely in family situations or around friends. They'll give sessions and tarot card readings for no charge out of the kindness of their hearts. It's not all about money. They're also about love and sharing their gifts.

The prophetic is a really interesting subject. Personal prophecy can encourage and bless people; it can provide direction. When you've come from a life like my own, prophecy is like a breath of fresh air. When you've been judged, rejected, misunderstood and maligned by people, you definitely need to hear what God thinks of you. Over a collection of hundreds of prophecies, I acquired an appropriate understanding and developed a positive outlook and perception of who I am to Jesus and to the Father.

I've established a personal and intimate relationship with Jesus Christ. So much of who I am today has come through the ministry of personal prophecy.

There are three main gifts of prophecy: word of knowledge, word of wisdom and prophecy. Briefly, I'll just share what each one is.

Word of knowledge is supernatural information about a person's past or present that isn't ordinarily known by the person prophesying. Jesus told the Samaritan woman that she had been married five times and now, she was living with a man out of wedlock. This was a word of knowledge. The person has to get their information supernaturally. You can list off certain character traits that God likes about the person, such as humility, patience, kindness, trusting, teachable or full of childlike faith.

If I was a stranger to you, and I named and explained five of your strongest character traits, you will know that my source is divine. How can a total stranger know all of these qualities of a person? It's simple. God speaks to the prophetic person and provides the insight into the stranger, such as a teachable spirit. Then, he has the prophetic person explain what a teachable spirit looks like in practice, so it resonates with the person receiving the prophecy. When I minister over video, I like to give about four to five character traits about a person to show them that God is clearly speaking so that they can then relax and listen with interest to all that is being said in the prophecy.

Word of knowledge can also be used in healing circles. A person can feel or hear about some type of pain or the name of a disease in their mind and can call out that disease in a public setting. They may say, "Someone here has a right ear that's always tingling, and they find it hard to sleep; stand up if you're that person." Most of the time, someone in the audience has that complaint, and if they stand up because of that word of knowledge, the healer can pray for them, and God will heal that condition. That's a word of knowledge; it's supernatural information.

Prophecy is information that God wants to communicate to a person. For instance, when you get a word of knowledge that says a person has a teachable spirit, the gift of prophecy can continue and say, "Because you have a teachable spirit, I'm going to move and use you to acquire a lot of knowledge. I'm going to give you revelation from my Bible and revelation from talking with me face to face. I'm going to give you dreams and visions. I'm going to lead you to books that will teach you some things that I want you to teach others. I want you to write a book and teach the people what you've learned." What I just said about a teachable spirit is all from the gift of prophecy.

Jesus can continue and say, "I want you to write books and do podcasts. I want you to write a blog, create YouTube videos and teach all the things that I'm teaching you. This is what I've called you to be — a teacher." That is a word of wisdom. It means getting directions from God through a prophecy. God is saying that he wants you to teach and that these are the ways that he wants you to teach or words of wisdom, in this example. It is totally up to the person receiving the prophecy to act on the words of wisdom. Many people run to get prophecy after prophecy and yet do not act of the words of wisdom that they are given. If you are not obeying God when he tells you what to do, it can delay the fulfillment of prophecies in your life.

In 2 Kings 3: 16-20, for instance, the king went to a prophet to ask about a battle and the prophet told him, "Yes, you are going to win that battle, but here are some instructions. When you get there, at the end of the night, dig a lot of holes and fill them up with water. In the morning, your enemy will think that your side had a fight in the midst of the night and killed each other. I want you to hide, so they will be unprepared for battle when they go to your camp. That is when you'll ambush them, and I'll help you overcome them."

Through words of wisdom from a prophet, they will receive divine strategy on what to do, and these instructions always work. That's a word of wisdom. Word of knowledge is supernatural information while prophecy elaborates on that information and provides you with further direction from God. Those three gifts most commonly work together.

However, discerning of spirits, deliverance and healing can also be used in the prophetic.

Chapter 2
Being Prophetic - What Is That?

Paul taught a lot on the gifts and in 1 Corinthians 14:1, he says, *"Pursue love, and desire spiritual gifts, but especially that you may prophesy."* Paul says in another place that a prophecy is the best spiritual gift. He also told us in 1 Corinthians 14:39 to covet the gift of prophecy.

Let's go through these three Scriptures and have a look at them in more detail. *"Pursue love, and desire spiritual gifts, but especially that you may prophesy."*

Paul says to pursue love. The prophetic is a way of life for some people. The ability to prophesy with these three gifts of the Holy Spirit — prophecy, word of wisdom and word of knowledge — really has a shock and awe factor to it. If you can confidently walk up to a stranger and tell them all about their life and their future, you command respect, especially when you start going forth in words of knowledge about them, information that you couldn't possibly know. You have their attention! They know within 30 seconds that you have a supernatural source for this information, and they're having a profound encounter. But Paul starts by telling us, even before we desire to see this powerful manifestation, that we should pursue love.

I have to tell you that since I've been operating in this spirit of prophecy for the last 20 years, *love is the most important thing.* You have to pursue Jesus and love because it's out of love that you receive all the ability, the unction and the motivation to prophesy. Many people think that a prophecy is like garbage and that most prophets give these broad and generic words that can be for anyone, so they don't respect the gift of prophecy. They think it's for lunatics and fringe people and not for the educated and wise. When they're talking about generic prophecies, they're talking about a person who has prophesied over them, stating something like this, *"You've had a very uncomfortable life, and you haven't always fit in,"* which is true of everyone. Or this: *"God knows your dreams, and he's going to step forth over the coming years and see your dreams are fulfilled."* You can get six or eight verses from the Bible and string them all together and make a very generic, positive-sounding message. But if that prophecy lacks the key element of words of knowledge and supernatural information about the person, it's not convincing.

It doesn't resonate with the person because nothing in it proved to them that it was divine. However, what happened to me tonight with a guy at Burger King shows you just how effective prophecy can be when it's combined with a word of knowledge and supernatural information. As I was leaving the restaurant, the Lord highlighted the man and told me to speak to him.

I normally say to a total stranger, "Excuse me, I have a gift and from time to time, that gift lets me get a message for a person. Today, I have a message for you." I gave that little introduction, and I went on to say, "You're a really kind-hearted person. You have a lot of kindness and compassion, and you treat people well. You're a good listener and encourager, and you have no judgment in you. You treat everyone the same — with dignity and respect — and I want you to know that God really admires that in you. He admires you for being the kind and compassionate person that you are."

The man said, "That's a really lovely thing to say about me."

I replied, "It is true, isn't it?"

And he said, "Yeah, that is true, but thank you so much for that."

I said "God bless you. Have a good day." All of that prophecy was words of knowledge. The person could tell that I seemed to know all about him.

The only reason why you'll give generic, bland prophecies is because the person prophesying lacks love and the courage to step out and give words of knowledge. Instead, they want to be recognized as a prophetic person. They want to have the status of being able to walk up to people and rock their world with prophecy. They want to be seen as a superstar who moves in gifts of prophecy. But they don't have the audacity or courage to say something that might be wrong on the spot.

What if I came up to a person and said that they were really humble now, but they were not always so humble and that the Lord had to put them through a few years of testing and refining so that now, they can be used?

If I share a prophecy full of a word of knowledge with a person, they know immediately that it's right. But if I told them this but had completely missed hearing God, they'd know immediately that I was wrong. They'd likely respond, "Can you leave me alone? That's total garbage."

It's very important to know that the prophet starts with true love because it's only love for your fellow man that lets you risk making a mistake.

God is quite able to speak to people and give them words of knowledge. But if the prophetic person lacks love, they won't step out and say the words of knowledge. They'll end up as part of the prophetic team, giving broad and generic prophecies. You can stand up in any church that allows prophetic words in the service, and you can string together five or six scriptures, and no one can say to you that your prophecy wasn't spiritually and biblically based. But if the Spirit of the Lord did not move on you and did not give you the earnestness to share those scriptures, that's not a prophecy.

That's just you pretending to be spiritual by sharing some verses. Many people step up and say eloquent things in churches when the Holy Spirit hasn't inspired them to do it. They just want to be special. That's why it says that the prophets are subject to the prophets. *Let two or three prophets speak, and let the others judge* 1 Corinthians 14: 29 (New Living Translation). It's a prophet who knows the voice of the Lord. I know when someone gets up and shares scripture after scripture in a so-called "prophetic" word. I know when the Holy Spirit inspired it, and I know when the person's own flesh got them out of their seat and had them boasting and trying to prove that they have a strong gift.

Broad prophecies without words of knowledge come from people who are scared and who don't love the person to whom they are ministering. Words of knowledge grab the person's attention as you're speaking to him or her. I normally launch into two or three words of knowledge about a person's character immediately to get their attention. Then, I tend to move into prophecy and words of wisdom once I have their attention, and they're solidly convinced that something supernatural is happening to them.

If I lay the groundwork with several words of knowledge, they'll pay attention to me when I tell them that God wants them to be a teacher and that he wants them to study and learn more. They'll listen when I say, "Spend more time in the Word of God because God wants you to teach people in the future." When I give them a directional word like that, the word of wisdom, they're more inclined to obey it because for the first five minutes, I, a total stranger, have just rocked their world, telling them all about themselves. So pursue love. Without love, you won't take a risk. The Word tells us to pursue love and desire spiritual gifts, but especially prophecy.

Some people boast and think that someone is less of a Christian when they don't have the gift of tongues. Well, I have the gift of tongues, and I can only speak one sentence in tongues. The gift of tongues has never developed in my life, so I'm embarrassed to pray in tongues in front of someone because I'm just saying the same gibberish sentence over and over again. I find power just singing a chorus in a worship song over and over. I feel more anointed and refreshed just singing the chorus than repeating the same line, but the average Pentecostal/charismatic thinks that they're supernatural because they speak in tongues. They have the gift of tongues because they got baptized in the Holy Spirit with the evidence of speaking in tongues.

Many people who have the gift of tongues speak in tongues very little, not even for half an hour. They don't have the discipline for praying in the Spirit for other people, praying over their life, requesting things from the Holy Spirit and praying these perfect prayers. They have the gift of tongues, but they don't use it like they should. If you have the gift of tongues, you should be able to prophesy. If you have the gift of Jesus' blood shed for you, you have access to God. Your spirit has been born again, and you now have access and ability for the Holy Spirit, Jesus and the Father to speak directly to your spirit. If you can hear Jesus speak to you, you can prophesy.

All you have to do is repeat what he says. Jesus may say, "Tell John that his boss isn't always going to be there, but he has to persevere in that job because he has to learn what it's like to be a boss who is under pressure so that he won't act like that boss in the future. Tell him to hold on — his boss will leave some day, but stay persistent now and learn how to be a better man."

If you shared this with John, it will really bless him. You might not that you've solved John's dilemma. You may not know that John was looking for other jobs in the paper, that his marriage was on the rocks because he's under so much stress, and that he was taking it out on his wife. The simple message that Jesus told you to tell John can have massive ramifications for his life.

You don't have to be Spirit-filled to move in the gift of prophecy. I was moving in the gift of prophecy and prophesying over people for years before I was baptized in the Holy Spirit. It's a fallacy that the gifts of the Holy Spirit can only operate when someone's baptized in the Holy Spirit. People who are not baptized in the Holy Spirit can pray a prayer of faith over someone and actually heal a person. They don't have to have the gift of healing. Their faith and a prayer can heal a person.

You can certainly repeat what Jesus told you to tell a person and prophesy. I was prophesying for many years before I knew that I had the gift of prophecy. I grew up as a Baptist and in the Baptist Church, they don't believe in the gifts or the baptism of the Holy Spirit, so I'd never been told what prophecy is. As a taxi driver, Jesus used to give me messages for people.

One day, I had a young, 22-year-old passenger who just came out of the pub, looking rough around the edges. Jesus asked me to tell him something. "Tell this guy to forgive his mom. She was hard on him and didn't bail him out when he was in jail, but she wanted him to learn a lesson. Tell him that Mom just didn't understand. People were bashing him up, and he really wished his mom taught him the lesson outside of jail by cutting his allowance or in some other way instead of allowing people to beat him up in prison."

The next thing I know, he's crying. I didn't lead him to the Lord. I didn't say a sinner's prayer. I touched him where he needed to be touched. He found the grace to go home and forgive his mom, knowing that she just didn't know better. A lot of people are making mistakes in this world because they simply don't know better. They're doing the best that they can. Mom thought that not bailing him out and leaving him in prison for a month until his court hearing was going to teach him a lesson and discipline him, but he actually was beaten up there and really hurt.

He felt betrayed by his mother since she left him in prison. That word really touched the guy. It's just an example of how Jesus can talk to you so that you can pass it on. When Paul says to pursue love and to desire the spiritual gifts, he's saying that we shouldn't stop at tongues but should learn to prophesy. The whole chapter of 1 Corinthians 14 tells us how much better prophecy is than the gift of tongues. If you read this chapter, he's saying that the gift of prophecy just walks all over tongues. He has an argument, and if we had about 90 minutes or if this book was twice as long, I'd go through the scriptures one by one to help you understand this point.

You are to desire the gift of prophecy. If you do, God will grant it to you and let you move in it. Desire the spiritual gifts, especially prophecy. Chapter 14 starts by comparing tongues and prophecy and says to desire prophecy. Since Paul tells us all to desire prophecy, which means that everyone can do it.

The second thing Paul said is that prophecy is the best gift. That means that signs, wonders, the gift of miracles and the gift of healings are not as good as prophecy. Why does Paul say that? Why is he asking us to desire spiritual gifts, especially prophecy?

You can learn how God feels about you and his heart towards you through prophecy. You find out who you really are and who you were created to be. You discover that you're special, dynamic, unique and that you have all these talents and abilities. Prophecy just revolutionizes your life.

After a lot of prophecy, edification, building up and encouragement by God from other people, you can go out and move powerfully in the gift of healing. You won't get there if you do not receive a lot of prophecies, saying that you're going to be a powerful healer. Prophecy is amazing. It is the best gift.

I said we're going to cover the three scriptures. Paul says to covet the gift of prophecy. In the Old Testament, it says in the Ten Commandments that you're not to covet your neighbor's wife, your neighbor's oxen or your neighbor's possessions.

You're not to covet your neighbor's donkey. In today's terms, that means that you shouldn't covet your neighbor's mode of transportation or shouldn't covet his car. If you see a car that you really like that your neighbor or friend already has, don't get jealous. It's so important not to be jealous or covet because it's one of the Ten Commandments, yet Paul says to covet the gift of prophecy. He says to go after it, want it and desire it with all that you have.

When you see someone with a very strong gift of prophecy, Paul urges us to covet that and seek God to have that gift for ourselves. There are people with a stronger gift than I, and I am always pressing in to improve my gift.

I can imagine that Paul prophesied a lot and built up a lot of people just like I do. I've given thousands of prophesies to strangers. I'm sure that Paul was always using his prophetic gift in conversations with people to open them up. Prophecy opens up people and acts as a conversation starter.

Being prophetic is as simple as moving in the gifts of prophecy. That's it. If you're able to move in the gift of word of knowledge, word of wisdom and prophecy; if you pray a prayer, and you have the gifts of prophecy imparted to you, then you're prophetic.

Many people have the gifts of prophecy but aren't prophets, and we're going to deal with that in the next chapter. Numbers 11: 27 tells us that Moses wished that all men were prophets. Moses was a prophet, and he wished that all men were like him. God didn't talk to everyone in the Old Testament; only kings, priests and prophets could hear from God on a regular basis, and so Moses wished that everyone could hear from God. We have the Holy Spirit that comes into us, makes us into a new creation and opens up our spirits to have our frequency tuned to God.

We all have the capacity and the ability to hear from God and to pass on his messages to other people. Moses, back in his day, was looking forward to the modern day when everyone who is a Christian would be able to hear from God.

In the future, I'll be teaching whole congregations how to prophesy and then take them out into the streets to prophesy to strangers. Then, we'll come back from the streets and debrief, and I will equip and build them up, helping them refine their prophetic gifting through training. I will teach all of the people in the church to be prophetic and mentor the people who are called as powerful prophets. I'll go from church to church, equipping people and putting them through courses to develop their spiritual gifts.

Prophecy is amazing. You need to be a prophetic person to be able to move in prophecy effectively.

If you want the gift of prophecy, and you're watching a video, a prophet can pray a prayer for you and impart the gift. Paul said in 1 Timothy 4:14, *"Do not neglect the gift that is in you, which was given to you by prophecy with the laying on of the hands . . . ."*

Jesus healed the centurion's servant by saying, "Your boy is well." He healed across space just from the spoken word.

The commander observed, "I tell my men to go and I say go here and they go here. Just say the word."

In Matthew 8: 10, Jesus then announced about the centurion, *"Assuredly, I say to you, I have not found such great faith, not even in Israel!"*

He had more faith than the Jews. Jesus healed across space, so I can just raise my hand and pray for you, and the spirit of prophecy, the gift of prophecy, shall come upon your life. If you're reading this book, and you want to move in the gifts of prophecy, put out your hands to receive and pray this prayer after me. Then go to my email address, and I'll teach you how to get into the anointing to prophesy, and then you can write and prophesy over me.

Once I hear from you, I'll give you feedback and tell you how well you did and confirm that you truly have the gifts of prophecy. Put up your hands and pray this prayer.

Dear Father, I recognize that Paul said that I'm to covet the gift of prophecy. I recognize that Paul said that I'm to pursue love and desire the spiritual gifts, but especially that I prophesy. I've always wanted to prophesy and so, dear Father, I pray that you would give me the gift of word of knowledge, the gift of word of wisdom and the gift of prophecy.

I accept that every good gift comes down from you and that you only give perfect gifts to your children. I agree with your Word that tells us that what father, if his son asks for some bread, would the father give him a stone? Or what father would give a bad gift to the child? I know that you're a good Father and that you only give good gifts, and so I thank you for the gift of prophecy, gift of word of knowledge and gift of word of wisdom, and I'll start to practice my gift and prophesy over everyone you'll lead me to from this day on. In Jesus' name, I thank you. Amen.

Now, you can go and put some worship music on and start to worship the Lord. When you feel the presence of God come upon you, like it does at church on a Sunday when you feel the joy, peace and the presence of the Lord, send me an email.

Type in my email address and write the following, "Dear Matthew, I have a prophetic word for you. Matthew, the Lord wants you to know . . . . " and then say the sentence that comes to your mind after you say "the Lord wants you to know." As soon as you type, "the Lord wants you to know," a sentence will appear in your mind. Just type that sentence and then as you're finishing it, the next sentence will come to you. Type that sentence and as you finish, the next one will come to you, type that sentence and around the third or fourth sentence, you may think, "I'm just making this up. This is just me."

That thought isn't yours. That's satan trying to stop you from prophesying. And just know that I'm a prophet, so I know when God's speaking. Even if you're just saying that God really admires, loves and respects me, and if it sounds really simple and generic, don't stop typing until you have a couple of paragraphs because I'm the judge of whether God's speaking, and I've never received a prophecy where Jesus said, "I love you, and I'm proud of you" that didn't make me cry. They're just simple words, but they mean so much when the Spirit of God is on them. Type those two paragraphs, put the title 'Personal Prophecy Practice' and send it to me.

If you've read this chapter and you already have the gift of prophecy, you can also prophesy over me by saying in the beginning of the email, "I already have the gift of prophecy, but I want to practice and prophesy over you." I'll give you detailed feedback on your prophecy. God bless and keep you, and I look forward to hearing from you.

My email for your practice is <u>survivors.sanctuary@gmail.com</u>

Chapter 3

What Is a Prophetic Person, and What Is a Prophet?

There is a difference between a prophetic person and a prophet. A prophetic person, as we discussed, is someone who can flow and move in the gift of prophecy. Many Christians have the ability to prophesy, but they aren't necessarily prophets. I have heard that everyone who prophesies will one day become a prophet. A lot of people would disagree with that statement, though.

After 20 years of prophesying, I find that it's easy to do. For that reason, I encourage everyone I meet to receive the gift of prophecy and to start to move in it. Prophecy is such a wonderful gift, and it takes positive steps in speaking life to people, calling out the gold in them, recognizing the beautiful things in a person, letting them know what God specifically thinks of them and stating the reasons why God admires them.

I find that many of my prophecies have the different characteristics of a person in them and what God admires about those characteristics. While my prophecies can be very inspiring, they sometimes lack in giving people direction, which is something that I'm working on. However, I do pass on everything that I feel the Lord wants me to share with people. Part of my prophetic gifting is growing, so when I say that I find it easy to prophesy, I am still growing in the prophetic gift. I don't think that anyone, even if they've been prophesying for 40 years, would say that they're not growing in their gift all the time. A prophetic person is essentially moving in the prophetic gifts, which is wonderful to have in your church.

I feel that many people in churches should be prophetic, and I aim one day to go from church to church, conduct seminars and teach everyone in the church how to move prophetically. I know that would really encourage the flock and every individual who visits the church if they had people who could tell them things about their lives and about what God feels about them and their future.

A prophet is called from birth though it may take many years before he realizes there's a call on his life.

In my life, for instance, I didn't know that I was called to be a prophet until I heard someone preach on the five-fold ministry. He went through each of the five-fold gifts — apostle, prophet, evangelists, pastors and teachers — and described the functions of each one. At the end of that teaching, I realized that I was called to help not just the non-Christians, but the people in the church. So, I decided that I must have been called to be a prophet.

I wanted to learn everything that I could about a prophet so that I could start to move towards what I was meant to do. I turned on my computer and searched for a chat room when I found a Christian site and registered with the screen name, *"Prophetic."* A girl who was also online asked for a prophecy from me, so I gave her one. She responded, "This is really amazing!"

I replied, "What?"

She reported, "I was just with my sick mother at the hospital, and I said to myself that I really to need to speak to a prophet. I went online, and you're also online. Are you a prophet?"

I typed back, "Yes, I believe that I am called to be one."

Many people mistakenly assume that they are already a prophet just because they have the gift of prophecy, and they're called to be a prophet. That's like someone in the first year of medical school calling themselves a doctor or in the first month of any long-term course of study acting as if they had already completed the program. When you get the gift of prophecy, it sometimes takes 10 to 25 years to develop in character, skills and abilities to actually walk in the office of a prophet. One of the big mistakes that young prophets make is to go around telling everybody that they are a prophet. A prophet may have prophesied about the calling to be a prophet on their life, but there doesn't seem to be much teaching about the 10 to 25 years that it takes to develop into the office of prophet. Their pride can get in the way and cause a lot of damage when they tell people that they're a prophet because people assume that they have experience but later find out that they have neither the track record nor the character of a prophet.

In his book "The Seer," James Goll mentions that there are up to 12 types of prophets. The last three he mentioned covered me — prophetic writers, prophetic equippers and prophetic evangelists.

I've written 14 books, and I am quite gifted in prophetic teaching, equipping and writing. Prophets can be very emotional about certain issues and want to preach on them in different situations. A prophet will discern what's wrong in a congregation, a city or a country and will preach the truth according to what they see. A prophet often feels strongly and can be very intense. They can be lonely, yet have an intimate friendship with the Lord.

Their intense passion for Jesus can sometimes keep them from having many friends. Although they desire friends, they don't want anything to do with the world and the lust of the flesh. They live a life that is separate from the world. Many Christians love to live with one foot in the world and one foot in God's Kingdom. A prophet can't stand that! They won't lower themselves to that level, such as talking about football or a current TV show all day. A prophet, in many instances, can't relate to people who are in the world and who are living a fleshy lifestyle.

Prophets have a mandate from God. Some are called to prophesy and have an impact on the nation; some are called to be a prophet in their local church and be available for people there. Some prophets are called to an itinerate ministry where they travel from church to church, place to place and nation to nation.

While there are many different kinds of prophets, they speak on behalf of God, not only as they release prophetic words but often when they preach as well. Their teaching carries a prophetic edge. On many occasions, they don't prepare a message, but the Holy Spirit speaks through them, and the prophet delivers a now word for the congregation that he's speaking to — a word that's immediately applicable for the people. It's not a message that's 2,000 or even five years old. A prophet will deliver a message that is needed that day. Even the sermon in that church the week before prepared the people for everything that the prophet has to say. All that has happened weeks and months before the prophet visits that church prepared the church for the prophet's message. A prophet would do well to listen to God and release only what God wants to say. Some prophets may have other agendas.

For example, some prophets may have a pet peeve or interest that they want to share. One of the things that I'm very passionate about is the parable of the sheep and the goats in Matthew 25 — I was hungry; I was thirsty; I was naked, a stranger; I was in prison, and you didn't help me. That message is very dear to my heart and one that I would share often, but I have to be careful as I start to preach in churches that I don't preach on that topic all of the time. I have to be open to the Spirit of God and allow him to direct me to preach exactly what he wants. A prophet should be led by God in what they say in every situation.

Many prophets are called on to give personal prophecy and do so with accuracy. Accuracy in the prophetic grows. It's similar to learning how to play tennis. A person begins as a young child and learns the fundamentals: how to serve, how to return a ball and how to do a slice. They may know how to do a drop shot, but a young child who's 10 years of age doesn't play at Wimbledon. You can see the talent in a young child and know that they have potential, but the child can't play professionally. That's how it is for someone starting with the gift of prophecy. They have the fundamentals down but can't be compared to a prophet who's "at Wimbledon," who's on the world stage and is highly accurate and very good at his craft, which is giving personal prophecy.

A prophet can develop their accuracy. If you're new to the prophetic, don't be too concerned when you miss it or hear things that turn out to be wrong. I still miss things from time to time and even with a high level of accuracy, I can be wrong. That just keeps you humble and dependent on the Holy Spirit. It's not just your own ego and personal strength that allows you to prophesy, but the Holy Spirit giving you the words to fill your mouth. It's interesting that someone with 20 years of experience can still get things wrong, but I thoroughly admit to you that from time to time, I give a word of knowledge that isn't accurate and get it wrong. Those instances keep me humble. I'm not endorsing inaccuracy in the prophetic, but in the ministry of the prophetic, people need the assurance that getting something wrong isn't the end of the ministry.

Many people quit prophesying because they get a couple of prophecies wrong, and the only one that wins in that scenario is satan. He shuts down good people, those who are going to be used to give thousands of prophecies in the future. They become discouraged after a string of wrong prophecies, so they give up on prophesying. Satan is very happy when that happens. The Kingdom of God, the Father, Jesus and the Holy Spirit are saddened by it, and sometimes, they can resurrect and encourage that person to start again. Satan hates the prophetic, and he'll use a person's lack of feedback to really harass you and mess with your mind. You may prophesy over someone and if they don't give you feedback, you start thinking that you got it wrong. You think they're not responding because you were off, so you are left thinking, "How did that happen?"

Your mind runs wild with all these thoughts that satan places in it, so you worry. It takes amazing strength to continue to pursue the Lord and prophesy. It takes great courage to prophesy over a nation or a church. Some churches allow a prophetic person to get up and prophesy over the church, which takes boldness and a lot of nerve. The Lord affords this privilege to certain prophets and prophetic people.

Some people move in the flesh. They get up at church and feel that God wants to say something, but it's actually their own agenda, so they release prophecies that aren't necessarily from God. This is why in scripture it says that prophets are subject to the prophets. In those circumstances, in a healthy church, the pastor and one of the prophets may take that person aside and say that the prophecy wasn't from God. "You missed it, and it might have come from your flesh. In the future, you come and speak to me before you deliver a prophecy, and I'll tell you whether you can release it or not."

Sometimes, a prophetic person, a prophet or the pastor of the church can step in after the prophecy and tell the church that those were not words from the Lord, but it will be highly embarrassing for the person. The pastor might also simply privately bring correction while still honoring the prophet who released the first word.

You can learn a lot from a prophet. They say that a prophet will often live out his message before he brings it to the people. He doesn't preach based on other people's books, revelations or their material. He lives out what he's going to preach and shares from experience. I haven't researched material for the 14 books that I've written. I didn't spend time reading other people's books to research my books.

I just sat down and made videos about the different subjects and chapter headings that I wanted in the book. I didn't depend on another's information. I simply spoke or wrote my books according to the knowledge that I possessed. A prophet should be able to speak from the things that he knows. He shouldn't be presumptuous or speak things that God hasn't placed in his heart. He should be speaking on behalf of God. Like anyone, you're allowed to share your opinions; that's what life is all about. But when it comes to other people, you should be careful not to act as if your opinions are equal to God's opinions. Instead, speak your convictions and the things that God has laid on your heart.

Are all prophets right? No, they are not. Prophets are always on a journey of discovery of biblical truths and theologies. Some prophets have wrong theology. Some prophets believe in a judgmental and angry God. They believe in the God of the Old Testament and don't understand that we're in a New Covenant and that God is best represented through Jesus Christ and his love. Some prophets are stuck in that Old Covenant doctrine and relationship with God. These prophets often seem angry and speak of judgment and doom. They emphasize the preaching of holiness, yet their own attitude can sometimes be unholy. However, the prophets who know and understand the grace message come across a whole lot differently.

You can share ungodliness in two ways. You can preach gloom, doom and fear, and tell people they won't see God if they're not holy, like it says in Hebrews. You can preach this scary message, or you can preach a message of grace that says that God loves people, and he wants everyone to go to heaven. The prophet can encourage people to live a holy life, a life dedicated to God. You can threaten people or encourage them. Those are the two kinds of prophets that are out there in the world.

Many prophets speak of judgment and say that God is an angry God. They say that he's furious with abortions, marriage equality and America. He's mad with this and that. Those prophets seem full of wrath themselves and don't appear to have a lot of peace. I understand these prophets simply because I was one of them in years past before I came into the understanding of the message of grace.

It says in scripture in the book of Revelation that a great angel will go and preach the everlasting gospel to the whole world. I believe that the everlasting gospel that the angel preaches is the gospel of grace, the same gospel of grace that Paul taught. I believe that Jesus will not come back until the gospel of grace has been shown and delivered to the whole world. I hope that I've given you some insight into this subject.

Prophets have many characteristics and will find it very hard not to be intense. I can be down to earth and talk to people about their TV shows and sports, but it's just like talking about the weather to me — very superficial conversation. It seems hard to find good friends with whom you can carry on deep conversations these days.

As a prophet, you have to lower your standards to have normal friends. According to what I have seen, many Christians can't endure talking about Christian things for more than half an hour at a time. I'm very close to Jesus. A prophet will be a friend to God, and God will speak and look after the prophet and be a friend to him as well.

Thomas Kempis wrote in "The Imitation of Christ" that if God really loves you, he'll want you as his own; you won't have any friends and only God will be your friend.[1] That's how it is for me. I have a couple of friends, but this saying

---

[1] https://books.google.com/books?id=5x9ULjz44FEC&printsec=frontcover&dq=imitation+of+christ&hl=en&sa=X&sqi=2&ved=0ahUKEwjb-8e99bTMAhUJQCYKHYUsCqQQ6AEIKjAA#v=onepage&q=imitation%20of%20christ&f=false Page number unknown, accessed April 29, 2016.

holds true for my life. I have Jesus, the angels and the saints from heaven as my companions. It is an enjoyable but lonely life. Prophets are rejected by many people.

It's easy for a person who disagrees with you to call you "false" because you claim to be a prophet. It's easy to be rejected when you talk about issues like feeding the hungry and the homeless and giving justice to people who need it. It is easy to be rejected when you talk about righteousness and Kingdom principles to people who are indifferent and who treat their faith with God as nothing more than an accessory. When you talk about matters of the Kingdom to people who don't want to know about them, you can be easily rejected. Prophets often seem weird, but the church vitally needs them. God used prophets during the Old Testament to turn a whole nation toward God when they were sinning and far from him.

Prophets today can come and speak at a church with authority, addressing every problem that's affecting that church body, really impacting them. This will greatly please the pastor because he can continue to be the loving pastor to the church while using a prophet to come in and speak the hard words that the church needs to hear. One of the best characteristics of a prophet is the ability to speak the Word of God. They can also answer problems, give direction, provide vision to a church and refresh pastors. They co-labor with pastors.

Any prophet who comes to a church, embarrasses a pastor and abuses his authority won't be invited back and is walking out of alignment with God. A prophet should be respectful to any pastor when he's invited to a church. Sometimes, God might call the prophet to speak to the church in a way that will prevent him from being invited back, but he has to be very sure about what God is saying and that his message applies to enough people to warrant being banned from the church.

I enjoy my life as a prophet. I dearly love the Lord, and though I am walking in the office now, I'm still finding my feet. I think that everyone in the Christian life is always going to be learning more about God and their purpose every day. I'm growing into my purpose, but a prophet is a complicated calling that includes a lot of grief, rejection, misunderstanding and suffering.

A prophet can go through a refiner's fire for many years, getting honed and persecuted by people while also going through personal traumas and sufferings. You can be used faithfully as a prophet only on the other end of all that polishing. God knows what he's doing, and if you're suffering, rejected, misunderstood, lonely and sad, you might be called to be a prophet and going through preparation for it.

You can learn a lot more about the prophet's life and ministry in John Eckhardt's book, "Prophet Arise."

Chapter 4
What Are Some Keys to a Prophet's Life?

This aspect of a prophet's life interests many people. What are some of the keys to the life that I live?

The Gateway to the Prophetic Office Is Found in Intimacy

One important key to a prophetic life is intimacy — an intimate relationship with Jesus Christ, the Father and the Holy Spirit. As a prophet, you should have a close relationship and a personal friendship with all three persons of the Godhead. They shouldn't just be individuals that you've heard about in the Bible. They should be your dearest friends. You should have interactions with each of them that you can use in stories and illustrations.

For instance, I was talking to the Holy Spirit, and I asked him, "Can you tell me when it's going to rain so that I can take my umbrella?" From that day on, the Holy Spirit was quick to tell me to take my umbrella every day that it was going to rain, especially if I was going to be walking from one place to another. Sure enough, if I ignored the Holy Spirit and didn't take my umbrella when he told me to, I got wet. That's an example of a time I talked to the Holy Spirit, and he responded and reminded me that it would rain.

I've had many interactions with Jesus that can't be summarized or detailed here. I would need a 100-hour video to explain all the conversations that I've had with him.

One interaction with Jesus was at the same place where I had the conversation with the Holy Spirit. I was walking out of my house, and I noticed the cloak of Jesus blowing in the wind. I normally notice him that way, and I said to him, "I'm seeing you now every other day." These frequent visions had been going on for a few weeks.

Jesus responded with, "I'm with you every day".

I quickly replied to him, "Where is that in the Bible?"

Jesus answered, *"Lo, I am with you always to the end of the age"* Matthew 28: 20. That means that Jesus is with us all the time whether we know it or not. That truth is amazing, and it really impacted me that Jesus was always with me. Now I know, whether I see him or not, that he's walking with me.

I've had interactions with the Father. One time, I was taken on a vision to heaven, and the Father had me sit next to him in Jesus' throne. The Father opened up the heavens, and I could see stars and planets and all sorts of things. If heaven had gravity, these would be crashing down into the Holy Land. Some of the planets or stars seemed so close. I could really see them moving. It was the most amazing view of the solar system and the universe that I've ever seen. The Father asked me, "Can you see all of that?"

I replied, "Yeah."

He responded, "I control all of it. I can send one of those stars to earth, and that would be the end of the planet. I control it all." He continued after a pause, "Don't you think that if I can control all of that, I can control your life?"

I was really emotional, and I answered, "Yes."

He stated, "Let me control your life."

This interaction with God had an indelible impact on my life. So intimacy is one of the keys to a prophet's life. A prophet has to have an intimate relationship with the Godhead — the Father, Jesus and the Holy Spirit.

Knowledge of the Word

A number of things make up intimacy. You have to understand who God is and find that understanding of God and Jesus through the Bible.

One of the keys to a prophet's life is knowledge of the Word of God. Many people think that they know the Bible, but they have a wrong understanding of some of the verses.

You have to understand that your relationship with God is ever-changing. Your beliefs and theologies have to be open to grow so that you can understand the Bible and the verses that help you to recognize who God and Jesus are.

You can find out a lot about Jesus by reading the four gospels of Matthew, Mark, Luke and John. Try to understand or seek Jesus in the gospels to explain why he did and said certain things and what he meant when he said those things.

You will come to know Jesus very well if you take the time to discover what he meant by all the parables and the deep meanings behind all of his commandments. You can study and spend time seeking the Lord with the help of the Holy Spirit. If you read the prophets in the Old Testament, you'll come to know God very well.

Having Two-Way Conversations and Asking Questions

Another key to intimacy and a prophet's life is found in conversations with the Father, Jesus and the Holy Spirit. I hope that if you're called to be a prophet that each member of the Godhead will speak to you. You will have to reach a stage where your spiritual ears are open so that you can clearly hear from the Father, Jesus and the Holy Spirit. One good way to really get to know each member of the Trinity is to ask Jesus questions.

You can ask him questions about anything, and he will answer you. However, sometimes he might answer that you're not ready to hear his response. Most of the time, the Holy Spirit is moving in your life and encouraging you to ask a certain question. If he inspires you to ask questions, then Jesus is going to give you the answer. I've spent hundreds and thousands of hours having two-way conversations with Jesus. I do sometimes pray like a normal person as in a prayer that ministers say in churches but only on rare occasions or when I get a specific request from a person.

Most of the time, communicating with Jesus is much like having a conversation. You can ask Jesus questions about his life on earth or ask him questions about anything and anyone.

Jesus only has good things to say about people. He'll call out the gold and the best in people.

If you are interested in politics, you can discuss the bad things that the leader of your country is doing. You may be interested in hearing Jesus' perspective on your current president. You may want to learn more about the New World Order and the Illuminati. Jesus can answer you and set your mind at ease on certain situations and subjects.

You can ask Jesus questions about anything. It's really one of the best keys and top secrets that I have to developing a deep and emotional relationship with Jesus Christ.

When you start dating someone, much of the conversation in the initial stages of a relationship is based on questions. You ask question after question to find out more information and slowly, you fall in love with the person based on your conversations and all of the information that they give you. The same is true with Jesus. You can get to know so much of his personality simply by asking him questions. If people wonder why they need to ask Jesus questions, here is what I say.

In the same way that you ask a date questions to get to know them better, you can ask Jesus questions. Jesus has real answers and real emotions. If you're able to talk to Jesus, you can hear him cry and express his feelings. You can hear his passion. You can hear his intensity about certain subjects.

Jesus is an amazing person, but the average Christian doesn't really understand or know him very well, probably because they don't spend a lot of time talking to him and asking him questions. As a prophet, you're called to represent Jesus and the Father. The more that you know him, the more that you know his characteristics and what makes him tick, the more you can speak his voice when he tells you to say things to a person or a church. When you have a better understanding of who Jesus is, you can carry his words more clearly because you understand the source; you understand where he's coming from, and it's not new to you.

People who don't have a good understanding of God, who only have an Old Testament view of an angry God, will speak on behalf of the God that they think they know. But if they communicated with God, they'd understand God for who he is. He isn't just some old man sitting on a throne with thunderbolts and lightning, ready to strike people dead and ready to throw judgment at any time. He's a God of mercy, love and compassion, like it says in 1 John. However, you might question that God is a God of love based on some of the things that some prophets have to say.

It's very important to know the Father, Jesus and their personalities — what their character is, what makes them laugh and what makes them upset. You'll see what makes them tick. You will come to understand that Jesus and the Father have their limitations. You will see that even though they're all powerful, they're limited by man on earth and can only move through men on earth. Because they are limited by men's actions, a lot of injustices can be stopped or alleviated by the Christians of the world. A lot of suffering in the world can be slowed down or even stopped if the Christians of the world acted and moved and weren't selfish, spending money on themselves and living a lifestyle of fleshly pursuits.

Once you get to know Jesus intimately, you know that every person is important to him. When you know him for who he is, you'll realize that Jesus intimately loves all the people in the world that others look down up — the prostitute, the pimp, the slave trafficker, the pedophile and the homosexual. It changes your attitude, the way you treat people and how you correspond with and interact with others online and face to face.

Asking Jesus questions will get you to this place. Reading the Word of God and spending hours and even years in the gospels will help you understand who Jesus is. Asking him questions about the gospels, what he was thinking and what he meant when he talked will draw you even closer to him.

Obedience

Another key to a prophet's life is obedience. God has called you as a prophet to be his representative, and that means that you should be listening to the commands of the Trinity and then actually doing them. I just released a book called "Great Cloud of Witnesses Speak" last year with interviews of 19 saints from heaven, what they had to say about life on earth and advice that they have for people here. It was very hard to publish because I came under a lot of criticism by many well-meaning Christians who insisted that I was practicing necromancy by talking with the dead. Most people know that everyone is alive in Christ and that those who have died are alive in heaven, so I'm not speaking to dead people. Despite the attacks, Jesus called me to write that book.

The Holy Spirit brought the saints down to be interviewed, and he was with me every step of the way. I could have refused to do this book. Jesus told me that two people before me had started the project and then stopped because of the criticisms. They backed out of it because of the pressure that came upon their lives. I was determined not to quit despite the pressure and the many reasons not to follow through with the project. I persisted and published the book.

It's important to obey Jesus. The disciples not only walked with Jesus but when he left, they obeyed the Holy Spirit and did things that the Holy Spirit directed them to, following Jesus unto death. They didn't consider their lives more important than the call of Jesus. We are called to obey Jesus, the Holy Spirit and to obey God in what he's called us to do.

You can't get close to God without a life of obedience, and you certainly can't become a beloved friend of God if you're not obedient. You won't have intimacy with him if you are not walking together, doing what he calls you to do. One explanation of a prophet's life can be found in Isaiah 42: 6-9.

I the Lord have called you in righteousness and I'll hold your hand. I'll keep you and give you as a covenant to the people, as a light to the Gentiles, to open blind eyes, to bring out prisoners from the prison. Those who sit in darkness from the prison house. I'm the Lord. That is my name and my glory I will not give to another. Nor my praise to carved images. Behold! The former things have come to pass. And new things I declare. Before they spring forth I tell you of them.

God says, "I'm the Lord. I've called you in righteousness, and I'll hold your hand." You have a very close relationship when you walk hand in hand with God, when you obey him and when you're walking in obedience and fellowship with him.

"Behold the former things have come to pass and new things I declare. Before they spring forth, I tell you of them." A prophet is in constant communion with God, and he tells you things and explains what's going on in your life. He declares new things as they come about.

It's important that you read the Word, talk to God and spend time in prayer. You need to ask Jesus questions and ensure that you obey his decrees.

Living a Life Set Apart for God

It's imperative that you live a life set apart for God. It is time for the church to live in a way that is different and for a prophet to live life in a way that is set apart.

1 John 2:15-17 (NLT)

Do not love the world. Do not love the world nor the things it offers you for when you love the world, you do not have the love of the Father in you. For the world offers only a craving for physical pleasure, a craving for everything we see and a pride in our achievements and possessions. These are not from the Father but from the world. And this world is fading away along with everything that people crave but anyone who does what pleases God will live forever.

This passage is calling people to read it, meditate on it and obey it to come out of the world. It's calling people to live a life separate from the world. Only a few teachings out there instruct a person how to live separately from the world.

It is one thing to say live a life set apart, holy, but it's another thing for people to work out how to do it.

James 4:3, 4 says:

"You ask and do not receive because you ask amiss, that you may spend it on your pleasures. Adulterers and adulteresses do not know that friendship with the world is enmity with God. Whoever therefore wants to be a friend with the world makes himself an enemy of God."

A lot of people are living a life of pleasure and lust, but the Word clearly lays out how we should live instead. One of the keys to living the life of a prophet is to live a life that is set apart, one that doesn't necessarily have the best that the world offers. Of course, a prophet visiting churches needs to dress nicely, and sometimes, a prophet will need a car and even a house. He'll need material possessions, but he's not consumed by them. He's not spending hours upon hours watching television and wanting to buy everything that he sees advertised.

A prophet that's truly called by the Lord will use his smartphone to post social media updates to encourage and challenge people. He'll use his computer to create videos and write letters and books. He'll use his television to relax and see what he needs to speak into when it comes to the things of the world. Everything that a prophet owns will be a Kingdom asset, a Kingdom tool and used for God's glory and not for his needs, lusts and desires.

One day, I'll write a book with a short explanation on how to live set apart. A part of holiness is to be set apart — to live not just a righteous life, but a life consecrated to the Lord. John preached it, and I share it as well, but not a lot of people do it. We heard from John that we are not to love the things of world. We read in James that if you're a friend of the world, then you're an enemy of God.

The ministers preaching in pulpits seldom show the people of God how to be set apart. If people will do it, if they remain faithful to God, concerned about him and his interests, the world will be a better place. The sad thing is that Christians seem to be just as caught up with the consumer mentality as everyone else. They are easily attracted to things of the world. They like to talk about sports, TV shows and everything outside of God. It's hard to find many people who can discuss Jesus and the Kingdom for hours.

Many Christians will recoil at what I just said. One of the things about being a prophet is that your whole life will be focused on God and his Kingdom. You will quickly dismiss anything that distracts you from it.

Being Set Apart With Friendships

One of the keys to having a proper prophetic life is to be set apart in your friendships. You can't have people in your life who drain you, pull the anointing out of you or suck the life out of you.

You have to separate yourself from people with a Jezebel spirit, cut them off and tell them that you can't have anything to do with them until they deal with that spirit. I have found that 90 percent of people with a Jezebel spirit deny it when you confront them. Unfortunately, they can't be free because they're not even aware of it. God would prefer you to be without friends than to have ones who drag you back into the world.

If the only thing that you do with a friend is talk about things of the world, then you must evaluate if the friend is worth your time. Isn't it better if you commune with God, Jesus and the saints of heaven and have them as your friends, rather than demean yourself and lower your standards to have meaningless conversations?

I'm glad that I am talking to people who are called to be prophets because the average person who does not understand these principles would probably think that I am too intense.

Worship

Another key to being a prophet is a life of worship. This does not mean just singing and listening to worship music, but worship is a life dedicated to Jesus. Your whole life and everything you do is focused on the Kingdom. Worshiping God calls for obedience as you live a life that is set apart, in constant communion with God. When you live a lifestyle of worship, your life is an everlasting fragrance to God. He can look down upon you as he looked down upon Job and brag to satan, "Have you ever seen someone so beautiful and so obedient?"

Living a life in constant obedience and devotion to God is a life of worship. You can learn to worship and play worship music in your house all the time. You need to keep yourself uplifted, walking in the Spirit and anointed so that worship music keeps the flow going. Worship involves more than simply listening and singing. You can live a lifestyle of worship as a prophet.

Chapter 5

How Do I Know if I Am Called to Be a Prophet?

It's not always easy to tell if you have been called to be a prophet. The process of understanding and coming to grips with your call can be short or long and arduous. For example, you can have someone speak to you prophetically and tell you that you're called to be a prophet.

Even one prophecy about your prophetic calling should be enough to convince you though that isn't often the case. God speaks to a prophet so that when you're growing up, you'll learn to hear from Jesus, the Father and the Holy Spirit. Hopefully, you'll develop a relationship with the Trinity.

My father's anger caused me to question God. I felt that God was angry, much like my father, and I feared approaching him. I had a friend who told me, "God loves you, and he's not like your father. He's not angry; you can approach him. He'll love and embrace you." My friend was crying as he related this to me, and I started to cry at the touching message, too. Some people do not have a good relationship with their father as they are growing up. Satan knows and desires these poor relationships, even causing a rift between a person and God. Satan certainly knew that I was called to be a prophet, so he made sure that my relationship with my father wasn't a good one. This caused me some difficulty in getting close to God.

I initially got connected with the Father by drawing close to his son, Jesus. He was no threat to me. Jesus proved himself to be a loyal and loving friend. Over time, with a little healing in my heart, I became so close to Jesus that he personally walked me into the throne room and introduced me to his Father, which improved my relationship with God.

Prophets are called to prophesy, which makes for an interesting life. When I prophesy to a person, church or country, it is often Jesus speaking through me, but sometimes, God the Father speaks through me as well. When we learn to speak on the behalf of God, we learn to understand his ways, love and character. The more we understand his character and grace, the more we can truly represent him in a wonderful way.

How do you know that you're called to be a prophet? Many times, a person who has the calling of a prophet sees things wrong with the church, sees injustice in the world and sees the church falling short of her call. Jesus told us to go into all the world, make disciples, baptize and teach them everything that he commanded his disciples to do. When you are called to be a prophet, you see that great assignment, and you compare it with how the church is operating. You can see a disconnect somewhere in the process. You can see where Jesus' commandments and directives to believers are falling short in the church.

You may open your Bible and read certain passages, compare the Word to the church that you attend and find a conflict since the church that you're attending isn't measuring up to the standards of the Bible. You may realize that your church seems to be off track and not aligned with the scriptures. The calling of a prophet is almost like a stirring in your heart, in your inner being. You sense that things aren't right, and someone has to speak out about the problems.

I find that I have a personal burden for the church, a personal discomfort and feeling in my spirit that things aren't right and that they have to change. This burden propels me to spend the time to make videos and publish them on YouTube. This burden allows me to start Facebook groups and equip people. And it's what propels me to write and publish books that will change the hearts of people.

I had a defining moment that really changed my life in the last few months when I was talking to Jesus about my reputation and not being known very well in the world. I personally have a message that I'd like to share with the world and yet do not have an audience that allows me to do so. Jesus said that he also has a message to share with the world, and he is limited as well. He said that he'd have to pick select prophets, teachers and preachers to share his message and choose hundreds of people. They'd have to give the exact same message to the people in their languages for him to have one congruent message going out to the whole world.

When I thought about it, Jesus has the same problem. He wants to speak to the world, yet he's limited in doing it. He can only use the ones who love him, listen to him and who will carry his message. As a prophet, you will have a burden on your heart that you have to share with everybody.

In Jeremiah 20: 9, the prophet summed it up by saying that he had a fire within his bones and that he was weary from holding it in. He had a burden on his heart that was inflamed, and keeping the message in drained him. God will place a burden on your heart that will grow and start to catch fire until you actually form the words and deliver the message. Only when you share the message will the burden be released from you.

Some people who are intercessors understand that God will place a burden on their hearts, and they'll have to pray for a person, an individual, a country or a church. They'll continue praying until the burden actually lifts, and they feel that the message has been communicated properly to the Lord. When the Lord hears their prayer, the burden will be gone. When you're called to be a prophet, you'll have the same burden with a message that is just burning within you to share. At the beginning, you might understand that you have a calling to the church, and then you get the message that you need to share with them.

I was given a prophecy about a month ago, saying that the burden that the Lord has placed on my heart will never fade. I will never be relieved of it, and it will continue to press me closer to the Lord Jesus and will encourage me to walk in an intimate relationship with him. It was prophesied that I will cry Jesus' tears and commune with God and Jesus in a fellowship of tears together as we care and love the world.

You might look at the five-fold ministry and see that you're not necessarily called as a teacher or as a pastor. You might see that you don't have a gift in evangelism, but you have a calling to give the church a message. You might not be an apostle, but you're called to be a prophet, giving personal prophecies and sharing messages with the church. Even when you know that you're called to be a prophet and that you have a message to share with the church, it is quite another thing to have the opportunity or a platform to speak those words to your church, community or to the nation.

The prophetic comes in three parts:

1. The burden that you carry

2. The message that you develop to share and

3. The platform or the opportunity to speak the message, which is totally up to God.

Many prophets, developing prophets or people who are being trained to be prophets carry these burdens for many years, which can make them a bit judgmental, cold-hearted or temperamental. They seem intense and frustrated and can be difficult people to get along with.

You might compare the situation to a person with a big load on his back who is trekking up a long hill; it's challenging and tiring. If you asked him if he is enjoying himself, he would probably look at you like you were crazy as it would be quite obvious that he was not enjoying himself. The grooming and training necessary to become a prophet is a long and strenuous process. As your character is fashioned, you learn to submit to God, to be humble, obedient and endure the refining of many other character traits that the Lord will bring out and manifest in your life.

If you feel called to be a prophet, you can ask the Lord for confirmation. Be sure to hang around prophetic groups or prophetic people, and God will use one of them to prophesy and confirm it.

I have a major caution here. You need to be aware of the big difference between being called to the office of prophet and actually walking as a prophet. The time frame can be anywhere from 10 to 25 years from the time when you learn of your calling as a prophet and when you actually sit and work in the office of a prophet. A brain surgeon must spend six years in medical school training to be a doctor and then go through additional extensive training to become a brain surgeon. After that, he or she goes through more training at a hospital in order to have practical experience in the field. A lot of years pass between the decision to be a brain surgeon and the time when he or she can perform their first brain surgery without supervision. If you compare the prophetic office to that of a brain surgeon, either one would need to spend 12 to 20 years in training before they actually practice. The same holds true for a prophet. You may have people prophesy that you're called to be a prophet, but it takes many years of training, humility, obedience and walking in the ways of the Lord, as well as lots of practice in prophecy, until you're actually trained and promoted into the office of a prophet.

When you are a prophet, you have more authority in what you say and do. A certain favor comes upon your life as it says in Psalm 1:3 that everything that you do prospers. You'll speak with authority and release a 15- or 20-minute prophetic word to a person and have that prophecy confirm many other prophecies that a person previously received. Your prophecy can sum up all of the prophecies they've had in their life. When you're in the office of prophet, you'll have such clarity, strength and grace upon your prophetic words that you'll have people stand up to listen.

Many people offer free prophetic words on the Internet and on Facebook. Other groups train people on how to release prophetic words or help people practice the gift of prophecy. These groups help us, and we all need them. Those new to prophecy may start their own Facebook group, but their words might not carry a lot of depth or strength or have authority behind them.

Every couple of months, I approach Jeremy Lopez, and he prophesies over my life. He provides accurate prophetic words that guide and impact me and make a huge difference in my life when it comes to making decisions and addressing relevant issues. I go to an experienced prophet, someone who is mature and whose words resound with authority and accuracy. He walks in a prophetic office. Up until such time, a person's prophecies might be correct and true, but they will lack the authority, depth and the clarity that someone who is in a prophetic office may have. You might work out that you're called to speak to the church, and you might get many confirmations through prophetic people that you're called to the office of prophet, but you also have to go through the transition, time and character development to become a prophet.

I imagine that many people start the process of refining and the testing of their character to become a prophet but eventually give up. I am quite certain that many people who are called as a prophet of God actually walk away from God and go back into the lust of the flesh and the things of the world rather than pursuing their Christian faith. The calling of a prophet and maturing into the prophetic office consists of extreme hardships and is an exceedingly difficult life.

Even though I'm in the office now, I'm still going through continual training, equipping and preparing for what God has for me and what he wants me to do in the future. I can testify that I have suffered many hardships, persecutions and afflictions to become the person that God has called me to be. You walk on a treacherous and narrow road. Jesus said in Matthew 7: 13 that wide is the way that leads to death and destruction and narrow is the path that leads to life. I'd estimate that about half of the people who are called into the office of prophet never make it, simply because of the hardships and the years that go into preparing a person to walk in the office.

Many who start the journey to be a prophet may not have the opportunity to walk in the office or to preach in pulpits.

They may not get to open their mouth and speak about what God has put on their heart for people. They may not have the chance to speak at a conference or for others to read what they have spoken over a nation or a city. They may publish a prophetic word over a nation on their own blog and have 50 readers instead of reaching the millions that they hoped to reach. The message in their heart may stay there for many years, and they might not have the opportunity to share it. These frustrating experiences can dishearten them. They'll go through all sorts of tests, including one for their patience.

God wants someone who doesn't call down fire on the people that he loves. God is looking for prophets who are full of grace, love, mercy, compassion and who remain unruffled in difficulties. He wants people who will respond to criticism by turning the other cheek and granting forgiveness — those who will move in love. He wants someone who can prophetically see an error in a person's life and help them correct it, not call out the issue in front of other people. These matters should be corrected by prophetically announcing, decreeing and declaring positive things over a person's life so that they can walk free from sin. A prophet should be mature enough to confront a church or country with grace and bring correction with humility and love to people and to the body of Christ, rather than confronting with a spirit of anger, fear, judgment and retaliation for all the hurts that they've personally been through.

If you have been rejected, misunderstood or even called weird, you may be called to be a prophet. If all you can think of and talk about is Jesus, if the world holds no allure and attraction for you, if you're totally set apart, there's a good chance that you are called to be a prophet. Many indications can give you a clue. To learn more about the subject, read more prophetic books.

More experienced prophets have a lot more to say on the prophetic and the prophetic office in their books. To summarize, you might know that you're called to be a prophet if the following apply to you:

1. If you get a message from God

2. If people have prophesied that you're called to be a prophet

3. If your life sucks

4. If you're misunderstood and rejected most of your life and

5. If you're passionate for Jesus.

You just have to hold on, go through the process, be obedient and do everything that the Lord calls you to do until you get to the point where God is using you. Then, everything that you turn your hand to will prosper. Wait until you have God's favor and authority in your life, and you'll reach a stage where people will take notice of what you say. People will be astonished at your words like they were when Jesus taught in the Sermon on the Mount.

Matthew 7:28, 29 (NLT) states, *"When Jesus was finished saying these things, the crowds were amazed at his teaching for He taught with real authority, quite unlike the teachers of religious law."*

When you're in the office of prophet, you'll be able to give direction and teach prophetically. People will stand up and heed what you say. Now is the time to obey, and one of the tips that I can give you is to learn to hear the voice of the Lord. Listen when Jesus, the Father or the Holy Spirit speaks to you and learn to jump when they say jump.

Do you know you can't simply receive the gift of patience? It is like a fruit that has to grow and develop.

By the time you get through the 10 to 25 years that it takes from a call to the prophetic to being in the office of the prophet, you'll learn patience and be an unshakable person.

Chapter 6
How Is Personal Prophecy Useful?

Let's talk a little bit about personal prophecy. Personal prophecy is a message from the Holy Spirit and heart of God to you. God wants to speak to his people. He desires to have heart-to-heart communication and share his thoughts, feelings and directions with you.

As a Christian, a person should concentrate on developing the ability to hear the Father or Jesus speak to them heart to heart. In the Parable of the Good Shepherd in John 10: 1 - 18, Jesus said that his sheep hear his voice; he calls them by name, and they listen to him. He goes on to say that the sheep won't listen to the voice of a stranger. Sadly, most of the church does not have the ability to hear Jesus speak to their spirit.

It's vital to learn this skill — far more important than it is for us to receive personal prophecies. I want to emphasize the need to learn to hear the voice of Jesus and stress its importance. When you receive personal prophecies, many of the words that are spoken will confirm what God has already directed or shared with you about your life and future.

So how is personal prophecy useful? Through it, you receive a true representation of your real identity in Christ.

God conveys your positive attributes, such as humility, a teachable spirit or a childlike faith, etc. You can be intellectual, passionate, driven yet insecure or you may be boastful and full of pride. Prophecies start to come to pass when God recognizes and is pleased with your humility.

These days, I personally try to avoid public arguments, but it seems that when you disagree with a Christian or present an argument that is hard for them to refute on Facebook, YouTube or in other social media venues, you can be accused of being prideful. Hearing a confirmation of my humility from Jesus helped me tremendously.

I started and managed a prophetic website with a team of six people that sent email prophecies to those who requested prayer to receive the gift of prophecy. I prayed for them and asked them to prophesy over me as a test so that I could provide them with feedback afterwards. Two-thirds of the prophecies that I received from the people new to the gift of prophecy said that the Father and Jesus love me and are proud of me. About 50 people out of the 300 said that I was humble. When you're living a Christian life, it is reassuring to be reminded by God that you're doing good work.

When God says that I am humble, it encourages, edifies and challenges me to become even more modest. I often interact with angels and saints from heaven as well as the Father and Jesus in visions. Many people have prophesied that I have a childlike faith, which is true. I believe that God is love and that he loves me and wants to show me things so that I can experience his Kingdom in a greater measure than most people. It inspires me to hear that I have a childlike faith because Jesus said in Matthew 18: 3 that no one will enter the Kingdom unless they become like a child. That means that I'm in the perfect spot for greater revelation and a greater experience of the Christian faith.

Christians need to know their identity in Christ to determine who they really are. Who does the Father say that you are? What does he say about you? What does he like about you? What qualities does he see that are beneficial and beautiful in your life? I know that God can speak to me for 100 hours straight. I run a Facebook group called *Prophetic Training Group,* and I asked people to listen for a prophetic word from God about two qualities that they see in me. Someone surprisingly asked, "Just two?" She stated, "God can speak for hours about the things that he likes about you, Matthew." That is true for each one of us. God loves us so much.

God will not point fingers at the areas where you're weak. He elevates you in the gifts that you have and gives a boost when you encounter a challenge. Prophecy, through words of knowledge and talking about character traits in a person's life, can rouse and uplift a person, especially if they are not aware of these characteristics. The person might not have really seen these traits about themselves or might learn of others that are revelations to them. A person might not think that they're called to be a writer, but when five people in a given year tell them that they're meant to write books, the person starts to get the message that God is calling them to write. So God sees things in us that we can't see in ourselves.

We're often so critical of ourselves. We're bound up with guilt, condemnation and insecurities that we can't see how good we really are. God is able to see past all the clutter and mess. He looks past the sin that you're in, looks right down to who you are and digs out the gold that's in you. He can reveal the beautiful things about who you are and what makes you such a wonderful person. Prophecy helps a person identify who they are in Christ and come to grips with the beautiful person that they are.

Prophecy can encourage a person to grow in intimacy with Jesus and the Father, which is central to the Christian faith. A lot of the gifts of the Spirit and power in the anointing come from a developed sense of intimacy with Jesus and the Father. It's out of this relationship that we develop strength and the ability to minister to others.

When people repeatedly hear that Jesus is proud of them and loves them, it's only natural to respond with intimacy. God draws close to us through personal prophecy. We then feel better and draw closer to God because of the exchange of information flowing from God's heart to us. It emboldens us to draw closer to him in deeper intimacy.

Prophecy helps to identify gifts, talents and callings in people. A prophet, or someone who is prophetic, can call out gifts in a person. You'll often see words of knowledge in people who have similar traits that you have, so you can call them out because it resonates intuitively with your spirit through the gift of prophecy. I have often prophesied over people who are called to write, which is one of the reasons that I've written a book called "Writing and Self-Publishing Christian Non-Fiction" that's available on Amazon. Writing fulfills me, and it's one of the things I'm called to do.

I've seen a vision in heaven of 50 books in a bookcase, and the Lord Jesus told me that those were books that I would write in my lifetime. I tried to sneak in to look at the titles of the books because I wanted to know what to write about, but I couldn't see them. Writing is my main focus in life right now; it's what fulfills me. I get a lot of personal satisfaction from people reading my books, writing reviews, writing to me to ask questions and thanking me for writing books. It's a major part of who I am, so when people tell me that I have more books to write and that God is delighted with my writing, I feel uplifted. One person told me, "Don't worry about the negative reviews you get. God has called you to write certain things, and he was speaking forth his words through you when you wrote the books that you did, so don't be afraid of what people say."

Those words took off a lot of pressure and worries over a few negative reviews that I received on one of my books.

I'm called to be a prophet, a prophetic evangelist, a teaching prophet and a prophet who equips people. When I receive a prophecy about what I'm doing, such as writing, evangelizing and utilizing the gifts that I'm given, I take it as confirmation that my life is on the right track, and I really am doing what God has called me to do.

Prophecy is confirmed as people move into the gifts and start to operate in them. As they start to find that they truly are gifted through prophecy, they find hope and purpose. If you start to move out in the gifting as prophesied, you'll find that God will give you the grace to move in that gifting. You'll find that it comes easier for you than it does for other people.

A person can also be told their ministry office. They may be aware in their spirit that they're called to a certain office, but a prophetic word helps them get over the unease, fear and the panic that sets into a person when they're called to do something. After they hear the prophecy, they will have the courage to go ahead and leave their place of work or drastically change their life to fulfil their calling. A lot of people need that encouragement to step out and learn or start to practice their gift.

Prophecy can give a person direction. For instance, I was directed to offer prophecy through a prophetic website. The prophet told me that I had a way of earning income that would enable me to finance the things I wanted to do in the Kingdom. So I started a website that provides prophecy for a donation that has paid for a few books to be edited and self-published. I used to have a backlog of books written, but I didn't have the money for editing or publishing.

This new website has opened up an income stream that allows me to publish my books. All of the money coming in has been because of a prophecy that gave me direction to step out and find a way to earn money. Before that prophecy, I had never considered going into business. I was on a disability pension and satisfied with the income although I wished I could earn more money. I just didn't want to go and wash dishes like I did before. I hoped that I would find a way of earning money that was enjoyable for me and that would let me publish more books.

I enjoy prophesying; it helps and encourages other people and provides a good source of income. I've had other directions from Jeremy Lopez through his prophetic words over my life, and I pay attention to the word of wisdom and what he directs me to do through the utterance of the Lord. You, too, should listen to the words of wisdom and direction that the Lord gives through a prophetic word.

A lot more things can be listed in this book, but I've mentioned a few key useful elements of prophecy. Delivering personal prophecies to people gives you a real sense of who God is.

When you share prophetic words, you feel his love, mercy and compassion. Soon, you start to think like Christ. You receive revelations from Jesus and the Holy Spirit. You begin to get the heart of God. You will feel compassion and love people just as God does. The more you move in prophetic circles and in your prophetic gifting, the faster you'll develop the heart and the mind of Christ. You'll grow in your relationship with Christ in intimacy, and you'll have a passion for God.

The prophetic benefits the people who receive it. At the same time, it enlightens and encourages the giver. Prophecies can be sent by email, video, text, voice messaging or on Facebook. You should also request a couple of paragraphs of feedback of how they were blessed and of the accuracy of the prophetic word. You will then find out how your personal prophecy affected them. I encourage you to buy books on the prophetic and learn all that you can because you'll have many years between when you're called to be a prophet and when you're actually walking in the office.

Chapter 7
Nine Purposes of Personal Prophecy

So far, we've covered prophecy and the prophetic office and the difference between being a prophet and being prophetic. Now, I want to jump into more detail about prophecy. We will cover 17 characteristics in two chapters, in no special order. I listed them as I sat down with a pen and paper and jotted them down, but I'm sure there are many more attributes than these.

I'm certain that Graham Cooke, who writes prolifically on the prophetic, could probably come up with a list twice as long as mine. You can find resources by him as he has a large prophetic ministry.

1. To Build Up

Many people in this world live under the weight of condemnation, guilt and shame. They habitually indulge in sin, which can bring all of these negative emotions upon them. It makes them think that they're no good, that they will never amount to anything and that they are never going to overcome the sin. It keeps people trapped in a cycle of despair.

Through a prophetic word, you can bring the word of God that speaks into that situation. You can speak into that person's life and build them up, just like a building that goes up level by level during construction. It might take a couple of years to properly lay a building's foundation. When people are trapped in a cycle of sin, their lives are founded on wrong truths, beliefs, scriptures and self-image.

In order to change, God has to revise our opinion about ourselves. He has to remove the lie and speak the truth in our life. The Bible often uses imagery related to battles. I see an image of a solider being shot and another one coming to pick him up, drag him to a shelter and stitch up his wounds. That's an image of being built up. God uses prophets and prophetic people to do just that — give personal prophecies to build up a person.

The prophetic builds up people from what they were into something new. Others often attack a person who is on top of their game and on top of the world, especially great speakers and those being used powerfully by God. They may get a lot of strikes from different directions. Hillsong Church in Sydney releases a lot of Christian music. The media often shares disturbing reports and says terrible things about them.

The attacks must take a toll on the leader, Brian Houston, and it would be wonderful for a friend or someone who knows him to write a prophetic word and send it to him the day after one of these news stories. A well-timed prophecy will effectively rebuild him.

If any of you remember "The Six-Million-Dollar Man" on TV, the theme said, "We will rebuild him — bigger, better, stronger than before."[2] They turned this damaged man that almost lost his life into a bionic man powered by computers and other technology. They rebuilt him. Many of us need rebuilding, too. The first purpose of personal prophecy is to build up a person.

2. **To Restore**

For an example of restoration, we can use my own experience. At the age of 14, I was on a beach and sexually molested by a 35-year-old male. He did things that surprised and confused me, but at the same time, my curiosity was piqued. My innocence was lost.

This led into a lifestyle of sin and a whole lot of issues. I was already dealing with other problems in my life. I had an angry father, and I didn't feel much love from him. I feared him. My life was already coming apart, but when the sexual abuse happened, my innocence was stolen.

If you have suffered sexual abuse, God wants to restore you through prophecy and say that you're pure, holy, humble, beautiful and special. You need to know that you're the apple of his eye. He thinks of you all the time. You're a jewel in his crown. You will hear a lot of words that will restore that innocence. A lot of people in this world have had their innocence stolen by the enemy. Sin is so easy to participate in. We live in a fallen world, a world where the lusts of the flesh come naturally to us. We can more easily

---

[2] http://www.imdb.com/title/tt0071054/ Accessed April 30, 2016.

indulge them instead of serving God and walking humbly before him.

Living a holy life without sin is amazing. You will not find many people doing it. Their innocence has been stolen, and they need to be rebuilt through both prophetic words and proper teaching. Correct doctrine about their identity in Christ can restore them. You can be used as a prophet to minister to someone and bring healing.

Many preachers fall into the arms of prostitutes, hide secret addictions or get involved in tax avoidance, tax scams and embezzlement. Many ministries have succumbed to the power of money and lust. Someone who has fallen so far might have been forgiven by God but can't forgive himself, so he will need multiple prophecies from prophetic people to tell him that God loves him just as much now as before he sinned.

He will need a lot of assurance from God through spending one-on-one time with him and through prophetic words to restore the relationship that he used to have with the Lord before he sinned. So many of us call these people false prophets or false teachers, or we heap blame on them, but they're sinners just like us. They deserve forgiveness and the grace of God. God can use you as a prophetic person or as a prophet to bring a word to a person to revive their innocence.

You can prophesy to someone who is beaten down, attacked, hurt or broken. You can deliver a prophetic word that will bring restoration in their life.

3. To Strengthen

You can probably imagine how prophecy has strengthened and encouraged me. To be told that I remind them of well-known prophetic people who I really admire and who have a great teaching anointing, a strong prophetic gift and a thorough understanding of grace lifts my spirit. I like to think that one day, I'll be a teacher, be well-recognized and be invited from place to place.

People are weak. They're weakened by satan, afflictions, the world, their jobs and the life they have to live. We live as weak and broken people. A prophetic word to a person can turn around that situation and bring strength to their character.

It can give them hope and faith. I received a prophetic word from a pastor once that I might have mentioned in another book. He said that the Lord had told him that I'd really suffered. Not many people understood my suffering even if I tried to explain it to them.

He said, "You suffered so much that it's caused you to think of taking your own life a few times, and through all of the suffering and pain, you never blamed God but still a question remains — Why me? God wants to tell you that the reason why you went through this without friends and why you suffered so much and endured so much personal pain was that He wanted to draw you close to him so that he was your only support.

You became really close to him because one day, he's going to use you to speak his words. He wants to be able to trust that you'll declare his words, no matter what he has to say."

That prophecy spoke a lot about my life and why I'd suffered. It answered why my life had been so hard. This pastor was able to say that God couldn't have achieved his goals for me any other way except through allowing this suffering to happen in my life for the greater good.

So here I am now, writing books, running prophetic groups on Facebook and speaking into many thousands of lives. I'm doing a wonderful and faithful job writing each book. One of my books has become very controversial. Even so, I can be trusted to bring the word that God wants me to bring. That prophecy helped to address the pain that I felt in my life.

I was hurt for years over all of the anguish that I had endured. I had a lingering question of "Why me?" I wasn't blaming God, but I couldn't understand why I had to suffer so much. Then I realized that this specific prophecy was given to strengthen me.

Just like a cast will be put on a broken bone to mend it and let it carry some of the weight so that the bone can heal, a prophetic word can align a person with the truth and heal him from whatever is causing distress.

4. **To Encourage**

I encourage people wherever I go and through whatever I'm doing because I have the spiritual gift of encouragement. It comes naturally to me. One of the main goals of prophetic ministry is to encourage others. I always see the good in people and therefore say positive things. To love people is my gift.

I was struggling once with a sin, and a prophet said to me that he saw a man beaten up on the side of the road, just like the man in the Good Samaritan in Luke 10: 25 - 37. God wanted that man to know that he's not battered and bruised in God's eyes. God sees his future, and he's going to be restored, healed and able to live a productive and successful life. That was a different way to share. It was such a beautiful message of hope and encouragement.

Even though this prophet could tell what my problem was, he delivered his message in a comforting way that did not overwhelm me. The message that I got was that God would personally come along the road, pick me up and heal me. If you're not encouraging people in prophecy, what are you doing? Are you prophesying for the sake of hearing your own voice? Are you prophesying to make yourself feel good?

If so, that is a trap. Many people start out in the prophetic and even continue for many years with wrong motives. They do it for what they can get out of it. They like the recognition from people as an anointed prophet. They like people's idolization and like receiving feedback about how accurate, profound and how awesome their prophetic words are.

True prophecy is meant to encourage people. One good way to measure if you've given a good prophetic word is to think about how you would feel if the same words were spoken over your life.

Would you like to receive that prophetic word? Would it encourage you? If you wouldn't want to hear that yourself, it probably won't encourage someone else, either.

5. **To Give Direction**

Many people are seeking direction. On one of my prophetic groups, I sometimes have people ask a question, such as "Should I move to Washington or to New York State? Option A: I'll go to Washington State. Option B: I'll go to New York State." I just ask them to frame the question and put A or B next to the available answers without telling me the specific answer. If I say 'A,' that means they should move to Washington State. So they chose to go there.

You can make decisions for people prophetically and give them direction or give them a choice to make. You can also help people through directional words of wisdom via the prophetic. If you're called to preach, God will give you directional words to immerse yourself in the Word of God. If you don't obey, you won't have doors opened for you to preach the Bible.

You have to familiarize yourself with the scriptures and get to know them really well for God to use you. Otherwise, no opportunities to preach will arise. You will wonder why you're not preaching, but if you look back on 20 or 30 of your prophecies, maybe three or four of them tell you to immerse yourself in the Word of God. When you find the answer, and you spend two years in the Bible, suddenly, the doors to ministry start to open, and your prophecies will start to come true.

God can give you clear direction through prophetic words. As I have said, I like to go to Jeremy Lopez from Identity Network who charges 40.00 USD for a prophecy. I have no problem with spending money on a prophecy from a distinguished prophet. He gives very clear and wonderful words with plenty of direction in them.

They confirm what I'm feeling and give me new direction for my life, which I like. Words of wisdom are part of the prophetic gifts and provide direction for people.

6. To Give Vision

Proverbs 29: 18 (King James Version) says that *"where there is no vision, the people perish."* Another way to phrase that is to say that people who have no vision will not prosper.

I feel that vision can be created in a person's life when God starts to give direction. For instance, I know that at one stage of my life, I'm going to be traveling and speaking at conferences and teaching workshops at prophetic schools. I'll be teaching people how to move in the prophetic, how to evangelize prophetically and how to bring prophecy to the church. Hopefully, I'll have a healing gift by then. I'll be teaching on all of the gifts of the Spirit.

I know that at least one of my books will be popular because I've had four individual people prophesy over the course of four years that they can see me on Sid Roth's show, "It's Supernatural." An appearance there would give me great exposure to others, highlighting my ministry, causing the invitations to flow in. Those prophecies cast a vision for me so that I have to prepare myself with enough books and enough resources and cooperate with the Lord on my own character so that one day, when I'm on international Christian television, I'm prepared for the ministry explosion that it will create.

The Lord is able to tell you through prophetic words that you're going to speak at conferences, travel the world and be a prophet to the nations. These are all vision statements that can be for 10 to 20 years from now. They create a vision and give you purpose and direction.

A prophetic word might help you hold on for 20 years. It can help you persevere and endure all of the heartaches and the pain and bear the refiner's fire until you actually see the fulfillment of these words. All of this will come to pass because you have this great vision of what you're going to do and achieve. I'm just a little person at the moment, but I'm excited because by the time this book is released, I'll have a total of 15 books published.

I have so many books just waiting for the money to fund and edit. It's like I have a production line of books within me. Even though I'm not recognized right now, many thousands of people are still being blessed and impacted by my ministry.

7. To Confirm Things

People often look for signs when they are about to make a decision. You can prophetically tell them about the decision and confirm that they are making the right one to give them peace of mind. You can speak about something that's been worrying them, and you'll bring a lot of peace and tell them that everything's going to be okay.

Humans sometimes lose direction when problems arise — that's just our nature. The more that bills pile up and the more financial stress that you experience, the less you trust in God and the harder it is to believe God when he tells you that he's going to provide a job for you. If a prophet gives you a prophetic word and says that the Lord's going to supply a job and open doors for you, stop fretting. You should have faith that it will come to fruition. The prophet is just providing remarkable confirmation of what God has already told you — in this case, that you will soon have a new job.

I have a lot of dreams and visions of my own and things that I want to do. One time, God spoke to me through a prophecy and admonished me, "You don't dream big enough, Matthew. If you imagine yourself doing it, how will I get the glory if you can achieve it in your own strength? You need to dream bigger."

I was already dreaming some pretty big things, and I laughed at what God said. I was sort of amused at him and wondered why he was saying that to me because I was already a big dreamer. But he apparently did not think that I was dreaming big enough. Through that prophecy, God confirmed that my dreams were going to come true. It says in Ephesians 3: 20, *"Now to Him who is able to do exceedingly abundantly above all that we ask or think . . . ."*

God will use prophecy as confirmation of many things. When you're giving prophetic words, you might be confirming many other prophecies that are being spoken by others. I remember one time when I went for a drive with someone. I'd already shown him angels after he asked about seeing them.

He saw angels doing somersaults, flying up into the air, marching with swords and spears, and doing a war dance like tribal Africans with spears and shields. The scene was very impressive to him. We drove for about an hour and had something to eat. We had a great talk on the beach. Then, he planned to drive me back into the city, about 40 minutes away. He asked, "Can you prophesy to me?"

I laughed. "Haven't you had enough? Hasn't all that happened been enough tonight?"

He replied, "I'd really love it if you could prophesy to me." I was anointed and had been up for a day or two, so I was very much flowing in the Spirit. I just started prophesying to him, which lasted about 40 minutes. At the end of it, he reported that I'd confirmed every single prophecy that he ever received in his life.

I not only repeated his prophecies and confirmed them but added information about each one along with more depth and clarity. He didn't have a recorder handy to take down my words, but that 40-minute prophecy was a validation of everything that he'd ever heard.

When you've made it into the office of prophet, you can give a 30-minute word to someone that summarizes a hundred prophecies a person has previously received. The prophetic easily flows from the anointing and the authority in your gift. Of course, it's God speaking! No stress falls on you. He's just speaking through you.

You just keep flowing and releasing the word without any effort. For example, when I teach in a video, I just speak as the Spirit gives me utterance. I have a cup of coffee while I speak point by point, and the Holy Spirit guides me. The same applies to a 30-minute prophecy.

8. To Heal

If you have the faith for healing, you can release prophetic words that heal people. You can declare to someone with a barren womb that they're going to conceive a baby.

You can speak a creative miracle to someone's womb. You can heal diseases and speak life. Don't just announce, "By Jesus' stripes, you're healed," but instead decree, "I speak to that cancer. Diminish and be gone in Jesus' name." While the exact language might differ, you can command demons and diseases to go in Jesus' name. They'll leave. While I'm not walking in a healing gift at the moment, I know that people can easily release healings through prophetic words.

9. To Give Impartations

I remember one day as I was walking from the train station to my church. Elijah came and walked with me. Enoch and Elijah are the two witnesses of Revelation 11. Both of them were walking with me and chatting, so I asked Elijah why I was meeting him so often.

He told me, "We're going to work together in the future. It's good to get to know each other so that we can develop trust and work well together."

I enjoyed his reply as we continued to chat while walking up a hill. He disappeared in a funny way at the end of the walk.

I asked, "Are you in heaven now?"

He replied, "Yeah. Did you see me go?"

I answered, "Yeah, you zipped up through the air."

He responded, "If you saw me go, then you have my anointing. You have my mantle." In the same way that Elisha received the mantle of Elijah, so did I. I passed that on to some world-renowned ministry leaders. They were very grateful and confirmed that they received that mantle. From time to time, when I see someone moving in a revival ministry, such as a ministry that helps people prepare for the second coming of Jesus, I'll impart the mantle of Elijah to that person, usually through a video prophecy. People feel it come on them as it starts to activate and move through their lives.

I also carry Joseph's coat of many colors. Jesus gave me Joseph's coat in heaven, so I impart his anointing of favor over people, too. I carry a couple of mantles and can also impart my own mantle.

If you have a mantle and have faith for it, you can impart it. I've even imparted mantles that I don't possess, but I've met people like Smith Wigglesworth and Kathryn Kuhlman in the spirit. They've been sitting in my lounge and listening as I've been prophesying. That's my sign to impart their mantle to a person. Most of the people that I impart mantles to give me feedback that they've felt the mantle come on them and have noticed changes in their ministry after the impartation. Along with mantles, you can also impart gifting to people. Those who do not have the spirit of prophecy or the gift of healing can still impart those gifts to people. They'll receive the gifts and start to move in them because you imparted it. Paul told Timothy in 1 Timothy 4: 14, "Don't neglect the gift that is in you, which was given to you by prophecy with the laying on of the hands"

Paul prayed and prophesied over Timothy and told him not to despise the prophecy but to hold on and wage good warfare with the prophecies that were imparted to him. You can prophetically release mantles over the lives of people. I hope that inspires you.

Chapter 8

Eight More Purposes of Personal Prophecy

1. To Create Something New

When God spoke, he declared, "Let there be light." There was no light, yet light formed in the universe.

God is creative. Everything that happens comes through our minds. First, it comes as a thought; then, we can create something from that thought. As long as God can speak and impart a thought to you, you can prophetically create something. You can speak about someone's destiny and create it for them through your prophetic word.

Although you can prophetically create a future for someone, it's up to them to walk it out. They might need to wait for years until they're walking in that word. I believe that even if the Spirit of God didn't give it to you, your spoken word can still create it. Smith Wigglesworth reportedly stated that if the Spirit wasn't moving, he would move the Spirit.

I believe that the spoken word in faith can create a miracle and a destiny that the Holy Spirit may not have inspired, but if you're in the prophetic and moving in the anointing, most of your thoughts and words will be coming from the Holy Spirit. The Holy Spirit will birth something in you, and you'll create it. I've spoken some really funny and amazing prophecies over people's lives.

Many times, what I've prophesied has taken root. The people confirmed that the prophecy was true and that it resonated with their spirits. That means I've created and started something.

2. To Give Favor

You can impart the gift of favor or the spiritual blessing of favor to a person. You can release the Psalms 1:3 blessing to a person, which says: *"He shall be like a tree planted by the rivers of water, that brings forth its fruit in its season, whose leaf also shall not wither; And whatever he does shall prosper."*

Once you release this scripture to them, whatever they turn their hands to will prosper from that day forward. You can take the favor of God that is on you and impart it to someone else.

Favor is amazing. All my life, I've been waiting for the favor of God, and it's finally starting to flow. A couple of months ago, I started a ministry where I receive donations for prophecy. I still have to work on getting my website up and at the right place on Google, but I advertised it a couple of times on Facebook.

I received $1,500 from people who wanted to bless me by giving donations. They received a prophetic word and then gave me $500 because they said the Lord told them to give it to me. That's favor! It has come into my life. I'm starting to believe in financial miracles and in the provision of the Lord.

I've never had faith for that before. I'm starting to see that as my needs arise with my book publishing, the money is coming in. Now that I'm moving in it, getting comfortable with it and know how it operates, I can impart it to others.

3. To Give Divine Counsel

There's nothing like having God speak to you. As I already stated, I've released 40-minute prophetic words on video. I really wish that someone would do the same for me and explain a detailed prophetic word with lots of description.

If you can tap into God and speak on his behalf, you can give people divine counsel. You can solve whatever is bothering them with just one prophetic word. You can solve their marriage problems or issues with their children. You can also give them hope and propel them to their destiny. Their faith can be restored in 20 minutes of God speaking through you.

If you record it, they'll have a chance to replay it later or to type it out, read it again and really press into the word. It will answer a lot of questions for them. The ability to connect with God, speak on his behalf and have him speak through you will allow you to release valuable divine counsel. You can't put a price on changing a person's life.

When I do the A and B exercise, I tell people to ask questions about decisions that they want to make or things that they want to know. They simply follow this process: "Am I going to be invited to preach overseas in the next year?" A is yes, or B means no. The answer came back A — yes, you're going to be invited to speak overseas next year. I once asked,

"Am I going to publish the "Great Cloud of Witnesses Speak" book in the next year?" The answer came back as A — yes.

I was able to publish the book within three months of receiving that word. I hadn't published it before due to the high cost of editing and because I was very concerned about the content. But I talked about obedience before, so I obeyed the Lord. I found a way to obtain the money through a government loan, paid for the editing and published the book. Prophecy can help with the decisions that you need to make.

You can counsel people about decisions, and they might not even be aware that you're making the decision for them when you give the prophetic word. People might write to you, asking about upcoming decisions. It's quite simple to ask the Lord and listen to what he says.

You just need to have faith that God will speak. If he wants to speak, he'll tell the person what decision to make.

It's actually a lot simpler than you think to help people make decisions.

4. To Confirm Other Prophecies

I mentioned in Chapter Seven that prophecy can confirm matters for people, but here, I am specifically referring to conformation of other people's prophecies. I sometimes give prophecies with a lot of confirmations in them.

When a person's just about to give up, when they've been put through the fire, God can use you to speak about a certain situation. They may be suffering intensely for so long; they could be waiting 15 years without seeing their prophecies fulfilled, or they might be starting to think that the prophecies weren't true and will never come to pass. The Holy Spirit may move on you when they are at the brink of giving up.

You can say the words that will confirm a lot of prophecies that they've had in their lives and the things that they were going to give up on. I really love giving prophecies even when they don't say anything new because I know that confirming prophecy is just as relevant.

Sometimes, it is even more important because it brings people hope that the prophecies will come true. If no one gives confirmation prophecies, all those that have come beforehand will go to waste because the person will lose faith in them. They need a fresh word to confirm that those prophecies are true. When they hear your words, it's worth a hundred prophecies. It will reestablish their faith.

When I recently received a prophecy about being on Sid Roth's "It's Supernatural," that gave me tremendous hope and a much-needed thrust because of the favor and provision that it will bring to my life.

By now, I've published quite a few books, and things are going great for me. When book writing and publishing were mentioned for the fourth time, I wondered what would happen in my future. People who give confirming prophecies bless others and fulfill one of the purposes of prophecy.

5. To Establish a New Thing

A person may have a unique perspective on life. They can experience life, church and the world, yet they don't see things quite the same as the rest of the church members do. They may read books, but they don't just agree with what the books are saying. Instead, they see something new — a different way of doing things. They embark on a new adventure. For instance, when I started a personal prophecy website 10 or 15 years ago, which offered free personal prophecies via email, as far as I know, I was the first person on the Internet to do it.

My site ranked number one on Google, number three on MSN and number two on Yahoo at the time. I received about 20 prophecy requests a day, started a ministry and recruited other people to help me. I was the first person to put it into action. Then Facebook came along, and I started a group called "Personal Prophecy Group" where you can request a prophecy.

I was the first one to successfully start that type of ministry there. I ended up turning the ministry over to someone else and stepping down. The ministry is still flourishing today, releasing thousands of prophetic words each year. If someone comes along and prophesies to you about being a forerunner, then you understand why you think of new ideas and new things. You have the task of opening or breaking in new things so that other people can follow.

It may not make sense to anyone else, but it will to you because you're wired differently. You've probably seen and done new things that you may not have understood. But when someone comes and prophesies that you're a forerunner and explains what that means, then you realize that you're not strange. You've just been created to birth new things into the world.

The elements may have already been present, but when you create something new, they will no longer seem unknown, frightening or controversial. I've had prophecies about being a forerunner in many areas and that I'll lead a lot of people into new ways of doing things. My book, "Great Cloud of Witnesses Speak," is a breakthrough book on interviewing saints from heaven.

I hope that many thousands of people start to meet saints. If this book really gains in popularity, it can open up a lot of possibilities for people. When you deliver a prophecy that creates something new in a person's mind, something that they haven't thought of before, they may instinctively jump on it and say, "Yes! Yes! That's for me!"

6. To Bring Faith and Hope

You can be used to prophesy over people to bring fresh hope and faith to them. The Bible tells us in 1 Corinthians 13 that the three best things that exist are love, hope and faith.

Hope and faith are incredible elements in a person's life. Faith is the ability to see things that aren't there yet or those that only exist in your mind. You create things because of your faith. Hope is the ability to hold on and believe in or for something. You can create faith and hope in people through the prophetic words that you minister to them.

7. To Let Us Know What God Loves About Us

I often receive prophecies about my character, what God loves about me and what I do. I received a tremendous prophecy today that said that I'm an exceptional and true example of a leader. The word went on to say that I'm the sort of leader that God wants in this world and that I will teach many people how to lead properly with authority and humility.

I thought that I was a decent leader but to have God say that to me is still encouraging. To think that I demonstrate the type of leaders that he wants in the world. I was just looking on Amazon for a person's book about leadership and how the model in the church is wrong and the next thing I know, God is saying that I am a good leader.

We should all lead as followers and servants of Jesus. I was interested in the book, but the writer's vocabulary was beyond me. I wanted the information that it contained, but I didn't want to wade through the difficult words.

I was upset that the book was not written clearly since I wanted to learn more about leadership. Then I received this prophecy that said that I'm already a perfect example of a leader. I don't need a book to teach me. I'm already leading like I'm supposed to. God loves this fact about me: I'm a great leader. He loves my humility and the fact that I can be taught because I'm willing to be wrong.

You can challenge me on anything that I say, tell me that I'm wrong, and I'll consider what you say. I'm happy to be wrong because next time that I teach on the subject, I'll be right. I believe every Christian is wrong about certain things and believes certain errors. We must all be teachable and open to hear opposing views and the arguments of other people.

We should not turn off our ears because we might find that we're wrong and they're right. I hope that made sense to you because God wants to tell us a lot of things that he loves about us. When I did an exercise with my *Prophetic Training Group* and had them list three things that God loves about each person, I was so encouraged and touched by the word that I received. The person replied, "Only three, Matthew? God can speak for hours about the things that he loves about you." She mentioned three and went into great detail about each point. Even so, she stated, "Honestly, God laughed when I sought him for the answer for this. Listing just three is hard because God loves so many things about you." Her word is not just for me; God has a lot of nice things to say about everyone.

8. To Confirm Our Dreams and Aspirations

You can speak prophetically over someone's life and confirm their dreams through your prophetic word. You can bless and change a person in a remarkable way. People are amazed when you can provide the details of their dreams, wishes and the secrets of their heart. People have told me, "You've been listening to my conversations with God. I can't believe you're repeating everything I said to him last night."

Over the years, God has refined my gift. You can also look up Graham Cooke for more information and other books on prophecy. Contact Jeremy Lopez if you want a prophecy or reach out to me at the address that I'll include at the end of the book to request a prophecy. In an earlier chapter, I mentioned that prophets often speak without a prepared sermon but rather speak as the Spirit gives them guidance. I was referring to this type of prophetic accuracy.

I had no idea that this subject was going to be two chapters long. It's simply the Holy Spirit giving me direction. Regardless, I think that Jesus can sit you down for five minutes and give you five scripture references in the Bible. You don't need 20 hours of preparation for a sermon to be anointed by God, but you can speak for an hour and a half from the pulpit on those five scriptures as the Spirit gives you utterance.

You can do that as a prophet who hears God, is close to him and who walks with the Holy Spirit.

Chapter 9
Nine Benefits of Personal Prophecy

We've addressed a lot of information about personal prophecy and its benefits. In the last two chapters, we covered 17 purposes of personal prophecy, and we may repeat some things here, but they are worth mentioning again.

In John 21: 15-17, Jesus asked Peter three times, "Do you love me?" Peter replied, "Yes, I love you like you're an endearing friend of mine." But Jesus was asking him, "Do you love me with unconditional, agape love?" Peter didn't understand that love until the Holy Spirit came on him so that he could grasp what Jesus was saying. The Jewish tradition uses repetition to emphasize important points. Between John 14 and the crucifixion, Jesus told his disciples, "If you love me, obey me" four times!

This repetition shows strong emphasis. Sometimes, a message bears repeating. Some people might even skip to this chapter to read this section. I want to provide a comprehensive view of nine benefits of personal prophecy.

1. It Is the Truth about You

All of the chatter in the world competes for our attention about who we are, trying to get us to form opinions of ourselves. For example, I'm overweight, and some people would even call me obese. I'm not sure if I'm quite in the weight range for obesity, but people judge you when you're overweight. The fact is that I've put on 30 kilograms, which is about 70 or 80 pounds, since I went on medications for a mental illness.

Nearly all of the extra weight is a side effect of one of those medications. But people don't understand that and ask me, "Why are you overweight?" They just assume that I eat too much or that I'm lazy and I don't exercise. While my exercise habits aren't the best, I often only eat one meal a day. My weight gain is not from eating too much. Nevertheless, people judge based on appearances.

People are driven to buy the best fashions and brands, whether in jeans, shoes or other clothing items. Women recognize a quality handbag when they see one. They know which shoes are the best. They make a point of following fashion news. They look at brand names that people wear. The world judges us on how we look, our income, the car we drive, the house we live in, the family that we have and how our family is dressed.

All sorts of voices compete for your attention. *"You're overweight. You're on a disability pension. You haven't worked for 15 years. You're a drain on society. You admit that you have a mental illness. You've only preached in churches five times in your life. Who do you think that you are, telling people how to exercise the prophetic and how to be a prophetic minister? Who do you think that you are, writing a book on a beginner's guide to the prophetic?"*

I've given between 15,000 and 20,000 prophecies. I think that qualifies me to speak on the subject of prophecy. I worked for 20 years to become a prophet and have matured into the office of a prophet. I'm working on my financial situation so that I can get off disability. I might be earning my own income soon. I am making progress, but only God knows the truth about me. Personal prophecy can tell me the truth that I'm not hearing from people.

I may hear the truth from close friends but not from the world. I'm not hearing it from acquaintances who don't know me very well. I'm certainly not hearing it from the advertisements on TV, radio programs and the news. They don't have anything nice to say about an overweight, mentally ill and disabled person.

When people ask me if I have a job, I reply, "No, I'm on a disability pension. But I am a writer."

They inquire, "How many books do you have?"

I tell them, "I'm just publishing my fifteenth book."

Many times, they react in amazement. They are really surprised that someone has self-published 15 books. People don't worry if you've self-published or gone through a traditional publisher.

The fact that your book is in print amazes people, but God sees all this. God doesn't look at what you are according to the world's perspective. Remember, in the Bible when Samuel went to anoint Jesse's sons and to find one of them to be the king, Jesse brought out all his boys. I've heard that in those days, the anointing oil was placed in the horn with a seal. Only the anointing of God released the oil.

The anointing broke the seal. Samuel tried to anoint each of the sons, but the seal wouldn't break. So Samuel asked, "Do you have another son?" The shepherds went to find David, who was just a young shepherd boy. They found him in the pastures, looking after the sheep. Samuel announced, "This is the one," and poured the anointing oil on him. The seal broke, and he was anointed as king of Israel.

1 Samuel 16: 7 tells us that God doesn't look at the outside of a man but at the man's heart. He looks at things that are unseen to man. When God looks at you, he sees your potential.

I've been to heaven a few times. They have movie screens, and you can sit down and watch a movie of someone's entire life and then watch a movie of their future — 10, 20 or 30 years down the road. You can watch what I've achieved in 30 years' time. When I'm talking to my sister, to Mary Magdalene or some of the saints who visit me from heaven, they've all seen the pictures of my future and know what I achieve. They've already seen what I will do and who I will become. They relate to who I will be in the future. When God sees you, he sees your potential and sees what you're becoming.

He sees the end product and announces that you're already there. He speaks life and destiny into you through the prophetic word. God told me a year ago through a prophet, "You're just so faithful." The prophet repeated himself over and over. "You're so faithful." I was in tears, weeping, and the prophet hugged me.

I was caught in sin at the time, so to hear God telling me through this anointed prophet, "You're just so faithful to me. You're so loyal. You're so faithful," broke my heart. God sees the real you. God shares the truth about you through the prophetic word. It may seem as though you never have any money, but God sees you as highly favored. You may think that there are no doors opening, but God sees the doors opening for you in the future.

You may not believe that you can be a best-selling author on Amazon, but God sees the day when you are. For a time, one of my books was number one in the prophetic section on Amazon as a top, best-selling book. I was thrilled! I have a friend, Praying Medic, who's written several books. They always reach number one as he has massive book sales.

Sometimes, I compare myself to him and think, "I wish that my books were selling as many as his. I wish that I was reaching as many people as he is." God has been impressing upon me in the last few weeks that my books are as good as his books. It's just that he has more followers on his blog — over 30,000 followers. Since he has a much larger reach than I do, his books do very well. But God sees the truth about me.

He made me realize that even though Praying Medic sells more books, he doesn't necessarily sell better books. That really fascinated me. He's saying it audibly in my spirit, but

God can tell you something through a prophetic word. And he told me that I am a magnificent writer.

I originally wrote the above words about Praying Medic six months ago. I now have a book at number one in its section on Amazon for three out of eight weeks. When I wrote the previous paragraphs, I was struggling as I compared myself with Praying Medic. I have since read more of his books, we are closer friends now, and he is one of the best writers that I know. I left my original thoughts here to show you how God can change your attitude and circumstances in just six months.

A lady prophesied over me a couple of years ago. "You're a really good writer, and I give you all the words that I've spoken, all the words that you've written in your books. Don't be afraid of people's criticism because I'm leading you in what to say." One good thing about personal prophecy — it is the truth about you.

2. It's how God Sees You

This is a bit similar to number one. Some people see me as lazy, but God sees me as remarkable. God sees me as able to produce the videos for a whole book in a short time. I have a book called "The Parables of Jesus Made Simple," and I recorded the 54 videos of that book by staying up for three days and three nights. Each video was 10 minutes, and back then, it took over an hour to upload and process each one.

That's 54 hours of uploading and processing time in three days or 72 hours. In addition, the videos took about six hours to record. Accomplishing that much in that little time is the work of a machine – not someone lazy! I had to be highly focused and anointed to be able to produce the first draft of a book in just three days.

I also transcribed the videos for this book that you're reading now. Half of my books are written and typed. Half are recorded on video, transcribed and edited. I write books in different ways. One famous author, Wilbur Smith, dictates his books into a Dictaphone. Then his wife takes the Dictaphone and does everything with the book from that point on. I said to myself before I started writing, "If I ever write, that's how I'm going to do it."

God sees the truth about me - that I am a machine. Some people, who disagree with me on Facebook or YouTube, accuse me of being proud. However, I've had about 50 prophecies that have told me that God is really proud of how humble I am. So I know that when people are saying that I am proud, it's because I disagree with them. God knows differently and tells me that I am humble.

People put a sword into me because they think that I am proud since I disagree with them. These people have a lot of scriptures to back up their point. They make clever arguments and use the Bible to support their views. When you disagree with them and they accuse you of pride, you might think that they have it right.

But when you have received 50 prophetic words that say that you're humble, you can fight those false accusations. I don't enter into many debates on Facebook. I'd prefer that someone buy one of my books. I then have 150 pages to convince them of my views instead of 150 posts on a Facebook thread trying to convince them.

I think Facebook arguments just inflate egos, but most people don't like you bowing out of arguments. They want to continue to debate. I've been there and done it as well. One benefit of personal prophecy is that you realize how God really sees you instead of what people think of you.

You can join me at the *Prophetic Training Group* and learn how to prophesy. This will give you practice and experience in prophesying over people.

If you are new to the prophetic, this is a great community to join and practice your gift. As you practice, you receive a lot of prophesies over your life, which is very encouraging. You can build up a collection of words to read on days when you are down. I have another Facebook page called *Author Matthew Robert Payne,* and if you look there, it's full of prophecies that have been spoken to me over the last three years. You can read the good prophecies that are coming in for me. If you wonder who I am and what right I have to speak about these subjects, look and see what God says about me.

3. It Can Be Trusted by Faith

At one time, I was suicidal. My favorite way to spend my days off was watching movies and eating all the pizza that I could. If a busker, or street performer, came to the city, I used to watch the busker play. One day, I decided to kill myself. I went down to the city to spend the day in my favorite way. I watched a movie and then went to an all-you-can-eat Pizza Hut where I bought a paper. I ate my fill while reading the paper for an hour, ate some more and then had some dessert. After that, I went and watched another movie.

I came out of the second movie and rang my former wife. "If I ever disappear and die, just tell Brandyn that I died of a mental illness." Brandyn was my son.

She asked, "What's the matter, honey?"

I replied, "That's alright. Just tell him. Will you remember that?"

She answered, "Yep." I'd said my final goodbye. I was on the way to a hotel to say goodbye to my friends.

After I said my goodbyes to them, I planned to have a few beers. Then, I was going to catch a taxi to a high bridge, walk to the top and jump off. I had it all planned out. As I came out of the phone box from ringing my wife, some singers caught my eye.

I passed a street band that was playing songs, including a song about holding on when times are rough. I can't remember the name of it, but the lyrics talk about not quitting when life is hard. It brought me to tears because I felt that the song was about suicide. It was really speaking to me, which made me cry. This guy walked up to me and said, "I see that this song has affected you. Can I pray for you?"

I swore up a storm at him as a big demon of suicide and death was on my shoulder. The demon used my voice to swear at him. He asked, "Before you go, if you don't want me to pray, can I just say something?"

I agreed, so he continued. "Imagine if I told you that you drive a taxi five nights a week and your favorite way to spend your day off is to get up at 11 a.m. like you did today. You came down to the city, and you watched such-and-such movie." He named the movie. He went on. "Then, you went to an all-you-can-eat Pizza Hut for an hour, read a paper and ate pizza. Then, you watched such-and-such movie." He named the second movie. "You've come out and rang your wife and said that if you ever disappear, just tell your son you died of an illness. Now you're on your way to drink and have a few beers. Then you're going to catch a taxi to the Gateway Bridge and walk to the top to kill yourself. If I told you all of that, would you think that God is speaking to me?"

Well, I was speechless! I'd never heard anything like that. As a Baptist, I grew up not believing in prophecy. That just blew me away. He added that God wants to speak to me further. He said that in order for God to say more, he would pray and then when he says, "Thus saith the Lord," God will start speaking. He asked again if he could pray, and I agreed since the demon had left because of the prophecy and the anointing.

He prayed, "God called you at an early age. You've been through a lot of turmoil. God promised you that you're going to reach out in ministry. Well, you are going to reach out in ministry. It's just that God needs to deal with a few rough edges first. When he has the rough edges dealt with, he's going to release you into ministry, and you're going to do great things and save the multitudes."

He concluded, "So just like the song says, you have to hold on." I was weeping. I share that story to say that a prophecy can be trusted by faith. That prophecy was given to me 20 years ago. While I'm still not preaching in pulpits, I've got my first invitation to travel overseas next year. The doors haven't fully opened yet, but I knew that he had that whole word of knowledge about my day completely correct.

Since he accurately gave me a word of knowledge, I believe that what he said about the future is completely correct, too. If you believe your prophecy by faith, you can hold on to it for 20 years. You can hold on. You can endure a lot of torture and pain and feel as if you want to kill yourself, but you will get over it and survive.

I used that story to illustrate that your prophecy can be trusted by faith.

4. It Inspires You in Your Walk

Another good thing about personal prophecy is that it inspires you in your walk. It's so encouraging to have total strangers prophesy about your future, all your dreams, aspirations and all the things that you plan on doing with your life. Total strangers can tell you what God says you're going to do. It's just amazing and will blow you away.

Sometimes, I wish that someone would give me prophecies that are as long as those I give to other people. I should ask Jeremy Lopez what he charges for a 40-minute prophecy. I might ask him to give me one sometime and offer to pay him $300. While I'm partly joking, prophecies really inspire you. They encourage you in your walk.

For instance, you can be very encouraged when you receive four prophecies that you'll appear on Sid Roth's show. One time, I heard a prophet share about an offer he received to minister on TV, but the Lord hadn't given him the go-ahead about it. He didn't do it and would have had to pay for that privilege. He explained that he waited two years and then had another offer to minister on TV. However, this time, it was going to be free.

This new opportunity gave him a lot more coverage throughout Australia and Asia, and they paid for him to be the guest speaker. If he had taken the first offer and paid for it himself, he'd always be doing so. Instead, he waited because the Lord said no. He declined an offer that seemed good at the time. But when he waited for two years, he got the offer for free. When he shared that, it sparked faith in me that one day, I would have a television ministry, doing great things and teaching a multitude of people.

So when different people prophesy four times that I'm going to be on Sid Roth's, it's brings hope for the first time that you're on TV with a lot of people watching you. It inspires me. I don't care if it takes a year, two years or five years for me to be on Sid Roth's.

I know that in five years, I'll probably have 30 books, not just 15. I don't mind waiting. I've waited a long time, and I can wait some more.

5. It Helps You Persevere

Many years before that man prophesied over me, saving my life and telling me that I would be raised up in ministry, I received another prophecy. I was at a Pentecostal church and went to a men's weekend at camp. This Pentecostal senior pastor had three other pastors and 300 people attending his church. He was our guest speaker. I had never been in a church with more than one pastor or more than 100 people, so I was impressed.

On the last night, he lined us all up and told us that he would prophesy over everyone. He planned to pray for us and told us that when he said, "Thus saith the Lord," that God would be speaking. About two months before this, I'd broken up with my wife.

He came to me and said, "*Thus saith the Lord, You're in a very dark tunnel. It's so dark, it's black. You're really sad in this tunnel. You don't think that there's going to be any light at the end of the tunnel. You're panicking because you're thinking that you will never come out of this darkness. I can promise you that one day, you're going to come out of the darkness, and God is going to heal you emotionally of your wounds. Then, he's going to raise you up into ministry, and just as Billy Graham was known throughout the nations, so shall your name be.*"

Now, that's the biggest prophecy I've ever had over my life, and it helps me to persevere. While a lot of that prophecy has come true, I still need healing in my life. The rest of it won't come to pass until I'm completely healed.

A lot of people think that believing in that prophecy is a vision of grandeur and part of my mental illness, bipolar disorder. One of the symptoms of bipolar disorder is thinking that you're the world's savior or that you're a new Jesus. You might think that you're going to be as big as Billy Graham, one of the most well-known speakers in the world, which certainly plays along with what doctors and others believe are delusional thoughts or the mental illness speaking, rather than listening to God.

I'm still not sure if my mom actually believes that prophecy or thinks that my mental illness wants to believe that prophecy, but I believe it because I was in that dark tunnel at the time. You see, the word of knowledge was spot on. I couldn't live without my wife. I was so broken-hearted and never thought I'd stop crying. In fact, I didn't stop crying until she remarried six years later.

I never thought that I'd come out of that dark tunnel. Now, I'm out of it, and the healing is progressing. I've had many other prophecies that said I'm going to go to the nations, and I'm going to reach the multitudes. One prophecy said, "You're going to reach millions of people." One prophecy said that I'm going to stop storms and earthquakes, and I'm going to control the weather.

One prophecy said that I'm going to preach all around Australia, throughout Asia and America and across Europe. I've received some huge prophecies, including one that says I'm going to be one of the major players in Australia's revival. Smith Wigglesworth said that Australia is going to start the last world revival. I've had other big prophecies that seem to confirm that prophecy.

What do I have to lose? I only need to have faith. The prophecy from 21 years ago helped me hang on through all these painful years with my bipolar condition and my suffering. Prophecy helps you persevere. I'm doing a lot less teaching and instead, sharing more illustrations with stories to show my points.

6. It Gives You Hope and Purpose

Prophecy gives you hope and purpose. I first discovered that I was a writer when I started writing poetry. I hit my wife one time because I was angry with her when we separated, so I slapped her across the face. I felt so badly that I wrote an exquisite poem for her to say that I was sorry. When I have to write something with a lot of emotion, I write poetry.

I took it to her at the police station where she was reporting the assault and obtaining a domestic violence order of protection against me. When I found her there, the police officer asked, "You admit to this?"

I told him, "Yeah, you can interview me now."

He replied, "We will." I confessed to what I did and went to court. A couple of years later, when I saw my wife, she opened her handbag, and she still had the poem inside.

Even though she was with another man at the time, I recognized the special paper that I had bought for it, which I saw in her purse. During that time, I wrote about 200 poems. Then, I wrote a novel based on nine of the characters in nine separate poems. That book was very dark, so I edited it for 10 years.

I planned to publish it, but Jesus told me, "You have to throw the book away, or you can't preach. You can either publish that book or preach." I dreamt of being a published writer because I was going to launch my career through a book so that I would become a household name. But I did what Jesus said to do and threw my dream away. Now, I'm a writer! It all started from a poem.

I have 15 books published, including this one, and five more that are written and waiting on money for editing. Prophecy gives you hope and purpose. Many prophetic words have told me that I'm called to be a writer with many more books in me.

I have shared this already, but I will expand on it.

I had a vision once that I was in heaven. I saw this bookcase with a lot of books in it.

Jesus told me, "They're your books."

I answered, "What?"

He repeated, "They're yours."

I heard the number '50' in my mind, and I questioned, "Are there 50 books?"

He responded, "Yeah, these are the books you wrote."

I tried to sneak a look at the titles on the books because once you have the title of a book, you know what it's about, and it gives you inspiration. But I couldn't see the titles.

About a year later, I had a dream that I found 50 golf balls on a golf course, so I took them all. I put it on a dream interpretation site, which is a bit like prophecy as others interpret your dreams. My friend interpreted the dream and said that the 50 balls stand for 50 books that I'm going to write. "You're going to write 50 books for the glory of God." Well, he did not know about that vision of books in heaven, so his interpretation was impressive.

When you tell someone that they're going to write 50 books, that's a huge call. Publishing 50 books means a lot of writing, editing and time. Someone needs to focus their whole life on writing if they want to publish 50 books. I had so much hope when he confirmed the number of books. I'm on book 15 now, so I know that Jesus isn't coming back next year.

He's not coming back in five years and probably not for at least 20 years. Even if I write three books a year, it'll still take 15 to 17 years for me to finish them. Jesus isn't coming any time soon, or he wouldn't have shown me the vision of 50 books and confirmed the visions through another dream interpretation with the 50 golf balls.

He wouldn't tell me all that and then not allow me to do it. In the meantime, I'm writing as fast as I can. I'm using the personal prophecy website as a source of income so that I can earn the money to publish my books. Even if I do my best, it's going to take a while to finish all of those books. My purpose for living is to be a speaker and an equipper.

I'm going to equip many people on how to move in the nine gifts of the Holy Spirit. I'm going to teach them how to walk in an open heaven and how to experience visitations of Jesus, angels, saints and manifestations of the spirit realm. I have received many prophecies about my purpose and am very encouraged by all of the prophecies about writing.

7. It's Personal Between You and God

When God speaks directly to you, you are blessed. Some people write corporate words where God speaks, and they release them every day. These words are good but don't apply to everyone. Other times, a word might be released for a Facebook group. Even when the daily words don't specifically apply to you, a prophecy over you is God speaking to you directly.

These words are just between you and God and the person who delivers the prophecy, who often doesn't fully understand it. You don't always have to understand what you're delivering to a person. You just speak what you're told and what you hear, and let the person work out what it means. Certain things are hidden from a prophet because if they really knew what it meant, they wouldn't prophesy it.

For example, a prophet can say, "This child isn't the last." The wife might have been hoping that her husband will come around to the idea of having another child, but he's adamant that one child is enough and that they are not going to have another one. A prophet can see a woman at a church when she comes forward with her only child. When the prophet tells her, "This child isn't your last," that sparks hope in her.

The prophet doesn't need to know what that means. Although it sounds right, he doesn't know the full depth of the prophecy or that there's a conflict with the husband. If he knew that the husband did not want a second child, he might not have the faith to speak because the husband is the head of the home. It would seem as though he's contradicting the authority of the man in the house.

Since the prophet does not fully understand what he's saying, he can spark hope to the woman so that she can rely on Jesus to turn the heart of the father. It's personal between you and God. A prophet won't always know what he's saying or the implications of his words. But when a prophet or a prophetic person is speaking, you're getting a message directly from God.

I like long prophecies of one or two pages. That's why I go to Jeremy Lopez. I have them typed out, and they're about two pages with extensive prophecies and full of wise counsel. I keep them all in a file folder, and I meditate on them. I do my part to walk out the action words. I follow the words of wisdom. I actively participate in bringing my prophecies to pass. Jeremy is really encouraging to me. When I give personal prophecies on my prophetic website, they are a minimum of nine minutes. If you have them typed out, they'd be more than two pages.

8. It Gives You Confirmation About What God Has Already Been Saying to You

Prophecy is one of the best ways to confirm what God is speaking to your heart. God might be saying to you that one day, you're going to have another best-selling book. You might doubt it, but God might keep repeating that your book will top the best-seller's list on Amazon or even on the New York Times.

Even if you doubt it, someone will prophesy that you're going to have a best-selling book. God confirms what he's been speaking to you in a remarkable way through a prophetic word. I have a friend who doubted my book, "Great Cloud of Witnesses Speak." He didn't think that it was going to be very profound or that it would apply to him. He told me that the first chapter when King David was speaking addressed three issues that God had been dealing with him about and really clarified the matter for him.

After he read about King David, he was convinced that the book was anointed and that it was a genuine message from God and the saints. It confirmed that he was meant to be reading the book. The same thing can happen with prophecy. You can receive prophetic words that encourage you to step out and do things that the Lord has been telling you to do. I had the same feeling about starting a prophetic website.

Jeremy Lopez gave me a prophecy that I would go into business. Since I could not figure out how to set up a tax-exempt ministry, I had to set it up as a business. It happened just the way he said. I've been able to publish six books from the donations that people have given to me via this amazing income source. I have so much favor flowing in my life.

I'm starting to see that God does supply everything when you need it. He can finance you and make you prosper. He can influence your life in ways that are tremendously exciting if you have faith in him and walk in his ways and do what he's told you to do! It wasn't until I started the prophetic website like Jeremy told me that I received 1,500 USD in donations.

For years, people could have donated to my ministry, but I never received donations until I stepped out. Prophecy can give you confirmation of what God has been saying to you. God has been telling me that everything's going to work out with the website and that the website programmers will successfully rank the site on Google — which is really hard these days — and not to worry about it.

God told me to work on my books and do other related activities. The staff on the website will keep my website busy, and so will I. Other people have prophesied that as fast as I write books, I'll be able to publish them with the necessary income. Everything is working out according to the plan.

9. It Helps You Walk on Water

The prophetic words in my life have encouraged me to step out and do the impossible, like walk on water. In the past six weeks, my income has increased from 400 USD per month to 900 USD per month. A prophetic word told me that God shall supply all my needs and that my income is going to match my book production. But no one saw that I could double my book production, and God would give me the needed income to publish those books. To an ordinary person who doesn't understand the provision of God, my prophetic words have me walking on water. I am doing so many things that are the work of the Holy Spirit. Who would believe that a person who failed English could write 50 books? But I am nearly one-third of the way there, and personal prophecy and a dream interpretation have told me that I'm going to write and print them.

In another personal prophecy, the person said that he saw a stack of books that were all written by me, again confirming previous words. Who would imagine that someone who got a 41 percent grade in English would be able to write a book? With that kind of track record, how can readers love my books and write reviews about how easy they are to understand and how amazing they are?

I'm doing the impossible, and so can you. Personal prophecy will help you to step out of the boat and walk on water and do things that are impossible, but you do them anyway because the prophetic word tells you to. It tells you to step out on water. You take that step of faith, and it all starts to work out. Honestly, nine months ago, I had no idea that I should start my own website and now, 1,500 USD has come in through donations.

That's not people paying for prophecies. That's above and beyond what they are paying — 1,500 USD in gifts. That's just marvelous, and it's paid for so much. It helped me publish three books. With that, God wants to do many more impossible feats. Ephesians 3:20 says:

"Now to him who is able to do exceedingly and abundantly above all that we ask or think, according to the power that works within us."

God can do the impossible through you. Do you believe it?

Chapter 10
Being the Light of the World

John 1: 1-12 says, *"In the beginning was the Word, and the Word was with God, and the Word was God. (That was, Jesus was the Word.) He was in the beginning with God, Jesus was and all things were made through Jesus: and without Jesus, nothing was made that was made. And in Jesus was life; and the life was the light of men. And the light shines in the darkness: and the darkness did not comprehend it.*

There was a man sent from God, whose name was John. This man came as a witness, to bear witness of the Light that all through him might believe. He was not the Light, but was sent to bear witness of the Light. That was the true Light, which gives light which made through Him, and the world did not know Him. He came to His own, and His own did not receive Him. But as many as received Him (Jesus), Jesus gave the right to become children of God to those that believe on His name."

The light that came into the world was the Word of God, which was Jesus himself. Through him, everything was made. He became the light of the world. It's fascinating that we're also called to be the light. Jesus says in the Sermon on the Mount, in Matthew 5:14, 15 *"You are the light of the world. A city that is set on a hill cannot be hidden. Nor do they light a lamp and put it under a basket, but on a lamp stand; and it gives light unto all who are in the house."*

This passage describes us as two types of light — a city on a hill that lights the whole night sky or a light in a house that lights the whole house. As prophetic people, we have to understand that we have access to the very light and glory of Jesus Christ — to become his light and shine like he does. Other promises in the Bible also mention light and shining.

Daniel 12:3, *"Those who are wise shall shine like the brightness of the firmament and those who turn many to righteousness like the stars forever and forever."*

Now, the firmament is the night sky. This passage means that you'll shine like the sun, which is our star. The sun shines so brightly that it lights up the whole day. It even lights up the night sky because it lights up the moon, which also reflects a lot of light to the earth. We're to shine like stars forever. Isaiah 60:1-3 also gives a promise to us:

"Arise, shine, for your light has come, and the glory of the Lord has risen upon you. For behold, darkness shall cover the earth, and deep darkness the people; but the Lord shall arise over you, and His glory will be seen upon you. The Gentiles shall come to your light, and the kings to your brightness of your rising."

It's time for us to understand that God wants his glory to be manifested in our lives.

It's not simply about learning to prophesy and becoming proficient at prophecy. You need to move in love — in a demonstration of compassion. Start to obey Jesus so much that you become like him, that you get the mind of Christ and that you start to walk like him. Many people say, "Well, that was Jesus. That's not me." But the Apostle Paul commands people a couple of times to imitate him.

In 1 Corinthians 11: 1, he says, *"Imitate me, just as I also imitate Christ."* The Apostle Paul was saying that he was like Jesus — that he imitated Jesus. Jesus was the light, and now the Apostle Paul was the light, like a sun shining the light to all people. When Paul says this, it's either massive ego or deep humility. Imagine saying, "Imitate me just as I imitate the Lord." I look forward to being in a position one day where I can say, "Imitate me. Just do as I do and do as I say because this is the way."

1 John 2:4 – 6 says, *"He who says I know Him (Jesus), and does not keep His commandments, is a liar, and the truth is not in him. But whoever keeps His Word, truly the love of God is perfected in him: by this we know we're in Him. He who says he abides in Him (Jesus) ought himself also to walk, just as He (Jesus) walked."*

John is saying that it's possible to walk in your life as Jesus did. Jesus was the light of the world and in the Sermon on the Mount, he said that we're the light of the world. He infused his light into us. We've covered a few scriptures about light. It's interesting that God wants us to be the light.

1 John 2:10 says, *"He who loves his brother abides in the light, and there is no cause for stumbling in Him."*

If you love your brothers and sisters, if you love the stranger, if you love people, there's no cause for stumbling in you. If you love God and you love people, then you won't sin. The key is what we discussed in 1 Corinthians 14:1, which states, *"Pursue love, and desire spiritual gifts, but especially that you may prophesy."* It all comes back full circle to love.

If you're going to be effective in your prophetic ministry, if you're going to be effective prophetically to people, you have to **ooze** love. You need to have love fill you right up and exude out of the pores of your skin. You have to sweat and ooze Jesus' love, as if Jesus poured his Holy Spirit into your heart as the living water, and the living water flows out of your mouth, out of your hands, out of you and refreshes people.

Jesus calls us to be a light and to light up the darkness. Light is something that we're attracted to as if we were lost in the bushes. If we saw a campfire, we'd head for it. We're attracted to light. As the world grows darker, Isaiah 60: 2, 3 says, *"For behold, darkness shall cover the earth, and deep darkness the people; but the Lord shall arise over you, and His glory will be seen upon you. The Gentiles shall come to your light, and the kings to your brightness of your rising."*

How do we demonstrate this light? How can we be the light of God? Well, we have to learn to let go of our self. We have to learn to submit to the commands of Jesus Christ, to get to know what his commandments are. Jesus actually gave us 50 commands. If you Google the 50 commands of Jesus, I've written an article under my name. You can easily find it in a search and read the 50 things that Jesus told us to do and not to do.

When we do them, we demonstrate that we love our neighbor and that we love God.

1 John 2:4 says, *"He who says, I know Him, and does not keep His commandments, is a liar, and the truth is not in him."*

John speaks directly and even harshly in this verse. He's saying, "If you know Jesus, and you don't obey his commands, you're a liar." You're lying!

If you don't obey his commands, then you don't know him because if you know him, then you'll do what he says. That's how we become the light. We demonstrate, practice, perform and obey the commands of Jesus Christ. It's important to understand what those commands are and to start to walk in them. John emphasized the commands. I mentioned before that between John 14 and the crucifixion, Jesus says to obey his commands four times.

John 14:21 says, *"He who has my commands, and keeps them, it is he who loves Me: and he who loves Me will be loved by My Father, and I will love him, and manifest Myself to him."*

These verses tell us that the person who loves Jesus obeys His commands! Who loves Jesus? John asks. He answers his own question — someone who obeys his commands!

John 14:23, 24 further states, *"If anyone loves Me, he will keep My words: and My Father will love him, and We will come to him, and make Our home with him. He who does not love Me does not keep My words: and the word which you hear is not Mine but the Father's who sent Me."*

Jesus is saying quite clearly here, "If you love me, you'll obey my words. If you don't love me, you won't obey my words."

This is more than just theology or just doctrine. It's a command. Jesus is saying, *"If you love me, obey me."* The demonstration of obeying Jesus is loving God and loving our fellow man. Some popular grace teachers say that the Old Testament has passed, and we don't have to obey the Old Covenant. That's good, and it sets you free.

But obeying Jesus' commands is sometimes even harder than following the Old Testament law. Following him means that you really love your neighbor and that you really love God. Truly, the world has not seen the drastic change that could happen if people started to love their neighbor. How do you demonstrate that love? Well, the parable of the sheep and the goats explains it pretty well.

Jesus tells us in this parable in Matthew 25: 35, 36: *"I was hungry and you gave Me food; I was thirsty and you gave Me drink; I was a stranger and you took Me in; I was naked and you clothed Me; I was sick and you visited Me; I was in prison and you came to Me."*

We sometimes forget that this is not just a story but that it tells us what will happen on Judgment Day. He'll line up the sheep and the goats.

Jesus announced, "What you did to me, you did to everyone," and they replied, "When did we see you naked? When did we see you thirsty? When did we see you hungry? When did we see you as a stranger and take you in?" Jesus says, "What you did to the least of my brethren, you did unto me." But the other people will say, "When did we see you naked? When did we see you thirsty? When were you a stranger and we didn't take you in?"

Jesus stated, "Whatever you didn't do to the least of my brethren, you didn't do for me." In other words, Jesus emphasizes a practical approach of living out your inward relationship with God. I don't hear this taught much. Most of the emphasis on being a successful Christian is reading the Bible, praying, going to church on Sunday and maybe attending a mid-week meeting. If you're really living for God, you'll give a tithe.

But no one talks much about obeying the commands of Jesus. No one talks about taking in the homeless or feeding them or feeding and clothing the naked or feeding the hungry. However, James 2: 15 – 17 emphasizes all of these.

"If a brother or a sister is naked and destitute of daily food and one of you says to him, 'Depart in peace. Be warmed and be filled,' but you not give him the things which are needed for the body. What does it profit? That's also faith by itself. If it does not have works, it's dead."

We need to be the light and to practically live out our faith. One of the good things about Graham Cooke is that he understands the love, grace and the compassion of Jesus Christ. He shows in his own life, in his character and in his own interactions that he loves people. He'll spend three hours in a church service prophesying over everyone in the building.

He doesn't have to do that. A pastor comes and watches the worship and then preaches for half an hour, and his job is done. But when a prophet comes to the church, he preaches for an hour and then prophesies for three hours — four hours versus half an hour. He doesn't need to spend that extra 3.5 hours. Even though it's expected of him, he doesn't have to do it. A good lawyer can earn 400 USD or more an hour.

What value should we put on breaking the chains of depression and suicide off a person? How can you put a price on a prophetic word that frees a person from addiction? What would you pay to see the prodigals come home? How much is it worth to see a person walking in their destiny, bringing thousands to Christ? The prophet releases all of that and so much more out of love. Not out of obligation.

Graham Cooke tells stories of staying with pastors when he's come out of his room in the middle of the night to go to the toilet, and a pastor has been sleeping in a sleeping bag outside his door. They want a prophecy from him in the middle of the night.

He just wants to sleep in the middle of the night, not prophesy. Jesus used to wake up with his disciples in the morning to find throngs of people waiting for him. He'd heal and teach people during the day. He'd then stay up until about 1 a.m., talking to his disciples, answering questions and doing debriefs.

The disciples had all sorts of questions. He'd answer them and put them all to bed. After about three hours of sleep, he'd get up. He'd go and pray for a couple of hours to get the anointing and the power to minister the next day. Then, he'd come out for breakfast with the disciples at 6:30 or 7:00 and start his day again. He'd spend another long day of ministry, going to bed at 1 a.m. and back up at 4 a.m.

Jesus didn't do any of that out of obligation. He did it because he was a servant to all. Jesus, the most anointed King of Kings, humbled himself to serve everybody. Now, people might be confused that I started a ministry, asking for donations for prophecy, but I ask for donations from strangers. I've already given 15,000 prophecies to strangers. Before this, I gave free prophecies for years.

I still freely minister to people and have done so for many years. You serve in ministry because of your love for people. You have to love the person more than you love yourself. The only difference between a short prophecy and a long prophecy is how much love you have.

I challenge any of you reading this book to sit down and do an mp3 recording or a video prophecy for me. Jesus can speak for three hours with a message for me. He has no lack of things that he can say to me. The only lack would be the time and the love you want to put in and sow towards me. Get a piece of paper out and ask the Lord to give you a five-page message for me.

I challenge you to do it. I bet that you can type out five pages and that the Lord just keeps speaking. I'm really good at activating people in the gift of prophecy because God has so many things that he wants to tell me. He's always speaking to me. He always has messages. He always has something to say to me because I'm always listening, obeying and doing what he tells me to do. He just loves talking to me.

You know what it's like when you meet a person, and they really love talking to you, hearing all your stories, and they ask you all sorts of questions? As you answer the questions, they ask you more, and they just love talking with you and listening to you. Jesus is like that with me. He just loves being with me. He loves me so much. He loves to hear me speak, and he loves to talk to me.

He loves to share his heart with me, to encourage me and get me out of worry and fear and to keep me in faith. He keeps me walking on water and doing the impossible. So I'm really testing the limits with certain things at the moment in ministry and business. God is making me walk on water, which is a bit scary and new to me. But God is continuing, through Jesus, to reassure me.

We need love. We have to practically demonstrate that love. When people see us in the world, they need to see love, light, compassion, mercy, kindness and self-control. How many people can't control themselves when others start saying something bad about someone? How many Christians chime in and gossip about people?

How many people jump in when there's a fight going on in a thread on Facebook? How many people read every post and laugh, "Hehe! He's really winning the argument," and add their two cents worth? I know I'm guilty of that. We're supposed to demonstrate love to this world. Personal prophecy is an amazing and wonderful tool, but you can't be a prophet without character.

Character is forged in love and compassion that you have for other people. If you don't have love and compassion for others, you'll grow up to become a false prophet. If you only want to serve yourself and your own needs, you'll want people to worship you and build a god unto yourself with a ministry to serve yourself and make yourself popular.

The difference between my business and how many people run a business is that all of the funds from my business are going into self-publishing more books. The money that I earn from my books also goes back into self-publishing more books. It still costs me more to publish books than I earn from them. But thousands of people have been touched by my free books on Kindle.

I'm so excited to have found a way to fund my books. I do it all for love and for equipping. Not for a big name because I don't have one. I don't do it to have a major ministry, either. I don't do it for prestige or for a great name among men. I only do it because I'm called as a prophet to equip people. I live to teach people how to prophesy, to train them how to be a better Christian.

That's my mandate. That's what I'm called to do. If you're called to be a prophet, then you need to teach people how to be a little Jesus. You should go around teaching people how to demonstrate Jesus to the world. I hope that I've been helpful. I know that if you watch the video of this book, you'll see that my tone is loving, and I have a smile on my face.

However, the tone of this last section of the book has become quite serious because this is a serious business.

My favorite writers are people who illustrate all of their sermons and what they say in their books with personal stories and anecdotes that come from their own lives. My absolute favorite part of a book is to read a personal story of someone's life, read their testimony and read the illustrations from their own life. I love people who are candid, honest and transparent. Some writers and teachers can't be that vulnerable.

Many prophets, before they're called, experience massive amounts of rejection. It's as if God were getting them ready to be a prophet and to be rejected for their message. God has a calling on a lot of people to be a prophet who experienced rejection before they were called and who continue to struggle with rejection throughout their prophetic journey. I'm happy to share my life, be transparent with you and let you know that we're all a work in progress.

I might have said some things that you might not agree with. That is okay. In the first chapter, I said that clairvoyants hear from spirit guides, and they believe that their ascended masters are human beings on the other side. I know that those human beings aren't on the other side and aren't giving them direction. They're familiar spirits, pretending to be a human with all of that person's information.

They might even appear and look like they're human, but they're not. I have to say that I understand because I talk to saints who have gone to heaven. I've interacted with them and had visions of them, met them, walked with them and talked with them. I've even had a saint manifest two times in the body of a person and hug me. Someone hugged me, and it was Mary Magdalene inside the person.

I've had some strange interactions, but everyone is seeking answers to their life. Everyone is seeking truth. Everyone wants to know their purpose for living. They want to be fulfilled. They want to be loved and accepted. They want to know what God thinks of them. The world spreads so much negativity through advertising, TV shows, magazines and Hollywood movies.

We receive all kinds of input from worldly sources. We're told that if your marriage doesn't work out, leave your marriage. If your wife is cheating on you, don't forgive your wife, divorce her. We're told that God is still angry and that he's going to judge America. He's going to pour out his wrath on the world. Many people preach this, and many more believe it. People use many hundreds of scriptures to back up those views.

If they don't spend time with Jesus and get to know him and the Father through the person of Jesus Christ and the New Covenant relationship, then they'll never be able to prophesy properly. They can walk in a measure of it. They'll never be able to walk in the fullness of what God has for them until their theology is right.

I'm not saying that my theology is completely perfect. I'm not saying that everything that I covered in this book was correct. However, I'm saying that I believe I shared the truth of my convictions, of what I believe to be the truth with everything I've said.

If you're new to the gift of prophecy, if you have the gift of prophecy and you want to practice on me, sure, practice away! If you feel the tug of the Lord to write out a two-page prophecy and really stretch yourself, I encourage you to do so. May God bless and keep you.

Closing Thoughts

If you have read this far in the book, I have to commend you. The calling of a prophet is no little thing. It is my prayer that this book will be only one of the scores of books that you read on this subject.

I pray that you will have the patience and the endurance to become the prophet that God has called you to be. I ask God to anoint you from on high, and I ask that the Lord draw you closer and closer to him.

Remember this. Some of the best journeys in life start with one step that seems normal. At the end of the journey, you take the final step that also seems normal. But the view from the beginning is not the same as it is from the end!

I challenge you to take that first step today and email me with a personal prophecy for me so that I can give you feedback.

Author Bio

Matthew Robert Payne has been prophesying for over 20 years. Over the years, he has become very accurate and given life-defining words to people. Although he has already written two books on the prophetic, "The Prophetic Supernatural Experience" and "Prophetic Evangelism Made Simple," Matthew felt led of the Holy Spirit to write a beginner's book on the prophetic for those who are very new to it or who feel called to it and are just starting out.

Matthew grew up in a Baptist church and was introduced to the Holy Spirit in an Assemblies of God church at 27. For the past 10 years, he happily attended a Salvation Army church until recently returning to a Pentecostal church called Catch the Fire in Sydney, Australia. Matthew lives to write books, to teach on the prophetic and to draw people into greater intimacy with Jesus. Matthew looks forward to the day when he is spending a lot of time leading workshops in churches and teaching people how to prophesy. Matthew sees his role on earth to equip other believers to become more effective witnesses for Christ. This book is written to that end.

I Would Love to Hear from You

As a writer, I welcome a personal email from you.

One way to really bless me, however, is to write an honest review of any length of this book on Amazon. This helps others decide if they should buy this book. Writing a review costs you nothing, and it is one way to let me know that you enjoyed the book. Please take the time to do so, even if you have never written one before.

You can email me and give me feedback, share your story with me or send me a prophetic word at survivors.sanctuary@gmail.com.

To read my blog, check out my other books, support my ministry financially or to request your own personal prophecy, you can visit my website at http://personal-prophecy-today.com.

If you have enjoyed my books and you want to promote them, please share the link to my Kindle book on Facebook and tell your friends. Many of your friends might decide to read my book when they see you post about it on Facebook.

How to Sponsor a Book Project

If you have been blessed by this book, you might consider sponsoring a book for me. It normally costs me between fifteen hundred and two thousand dollars or more to produce each book that I write, depending on the length of the book.

If you seek the Holy Spirit about financing a book for me, I know that the Lord would be eternally grateful to you. Consider how much this book has blessed you and then think of hundreds or even thousands of people who would be blessed by a book of mine. As you are probably aware, the vast majority of my books are ninety-nine cents on Kindle, which proves to you that book writing is indeed a ministry for me and not a money- making venture. I would be very happy if you supported me in this.

If you have any questions for me or if you want to know what projects I am currently working on that your money might finance, you can write to me at survivors.sanctuary@gmail.com and ask me for more information. I would be pleased to give you more details about my projects. You can sow any amount to my ministry by simply sending me money via the PayPal link at this address: http://personal-prophecy-today.com/support-my-ministry/ You can be sure that your support, no matter the amount, will be used for the publishing of helpful Christian books for people to read.

Other Books by Matthew Robert Payne

The Parables of Jesus Made Simple

The Prophetic Supernatural Experience

Prophetic Evangelism Made Simple

Your Identity in Christ

His Redeeming Love- A Memoir

Writing and Self-Publishing Christian Nonfiction

Coping With Your Pain and Suffering

Living for Eternity

Jesus Speaking Today

Great Cloud of Witnesses Speak

My Radical Encounters With Angels

Finding Intimacy With Jesus Made Simple

My Radical Encounters With Angels- Book Two

Coming Soon:

Michael Jackson Speaks from Heaven: A Divine Revelation, tentatively scheduled for release May 30.

Conversations with God

7 Keys to Intimacy with Jesus

Go Into All the World

You can find my published books on my Amazon author page here:

http://tinyurl.com/jq3h893

www.ingramcontent.com/pod-product-compliance
Lightning Source LLC
Chambersburg PA
CBHW072048290426
44110CB00014B/1590